Date Due

MAR 13			
MAR 26			
MAR 3 2009			
FEB 10 2010			

BRODART, CO. Cat. No. 23-233-003 Printed in U.S.A.

Exploring Gun Use in America

Titles in the series

VOLUME 1
The Second Amendment

VOLUME 2
The Firearms Industry

VOLUME 3
Children and Guns

VOLUME 4
Public Opinion

Exploring Gun Use in America

VOLUME 1
The Second Amendment

GREENWOOD PRESS
Westport, Connecticut • London

Library of Congress Cataloging-in-Publication Data

Exploring gun use in America / Creative Media Applications.
p. cm. – (Middle school reference)
Includes bibliographical references and index.
Contents: v. 1. The second amendment – v. 2. The firearms industry – v. 3. Children and guns – v. 4. Public opinion.
ISBN 0-313-32896-X (alk. paper: set) – ISBN 0-313-32897-8 (alk. paper: vol. 1) – ISBN 0-313-32898-6 (alk. paper: vol. 2) – ISBN 0-313-32899-4 (alk. paper: vol. 3) – ISBN 0-313-32900-1 (alk. paper: vol. 4)
1. Gun control – United States. 2. Firearms – Law and legislation – United States. 3. Gun control – United States – Public opinion. 4. Public opinion – United States. I. Creative Media Applications. II. Series.
HV7436.E94 2004
363.33'0973 – dc22 2003067750

British Library Cataloguing in Publication Data is available.

Library of Congress Catalog Card Number: 2003067750
ISBN: 0-313-32896-X (set)
0-313-32897-8 (vol. 1)
0-313-32898-6 (vol. 2)
0-313-32899-4 (vol. 3)
0-313-32900-1 (vol. 4)

First published in 2004

Greenwood Press, 88 Post Road West, Westport, CT 06881
An imprint of Greenwood Publishing Group, Inc.
www.greenwood.com

Printed in the United States of America

The paper used in this book complies with the Permanent Paper Standard issued by the National Information Standards Organization (Z39.48-1984).

10 9 8 7 6 5 4 3 2 1

A Creative Media Applications, Inc. Production
WRITER: Mathew Kachur
DESIGN AND PRODUCTION: Alan Barnett, Inc.
EDITOR: Matt Levine
COPYEDITOR: Laurie Lieb
PROOFREADER: Betty Pessagno
INDEXER: Nara Wood
ASSOCIATED PRESS PHOTO RESEARCHER: Yvette Reyes
CONSULTANT: Eugene Volokh, Professor of Law, UCLA School of Law

PHOTO CREDITS:
AP/Wide World Photographs *pages:* ix, xi, xii, 21, 26, 59, 63, 65, 66, 70, 73, 77, 80, 83, 89, 90, 92, 95, 100, 103, 114,
© Hulton Archives/Getty Images *pages:* 1, 3, 7, 10, 12, 15, 16, 18, 23, 28, 31, 33, 39, 44, 51, 54, 56, 85, 105, 109, 111
© Bettmann/CORBIS *page:* 4
© CORBIS *page:* 9, 43

Table of Contents

	viii	Introduction
Chapter 1	**1**	The Right to Bear Arms Before the Constitution
Chapter 2	**21**	The Creation of the Second Amendment
Chapter 3	**39**	Guns and the Militia in American Culture
Chapter 4	**63**	Gun Control Legislation and the Right to Keep and Bear Arms
Chapter 5	**83**	The Modern Debate over the Second Amendment
Chapter 6	**103**	The Judicial View of the Second Amendment
	120	Glossary
	122	Bibliography
	123	Index

INTRODUCTION

On April 20, 1999, two teenage students armed with explosives and four guns walked into Columbine High School in Littleton, Colorado. Firing their guns just as they had carefully planned at home, they killed twelve students and one teacher. They also wounded twenty-three other students before killing themselves. The previous ten years had seen several bloody shootings in American schools, but this was the worst in U.S. history. Every time an incident like this occurs, the role of guns in American society becomes the subject of widespread public debate.

The creators of the U.S. Constitution tried to address the issue of firearms in the Second Amendment. The Second Amendment was added to the Constitution in 1791 as part of a group of ten amendments known as the Bill of Rights. (An *amendment* is a change or addition to a legal document.) Like most of these amendments, the wording of the Second Amendment is brief. It consists of only one sentence, of twenty-seven words, which states: "A well regulated militia, being necessary to the security of a free State, the right of the people to keep and bear arms, shall not be infringed."

Because the Second Amendment is so short and its phrasing so peculiar, it has been the subject of enormous controversy. The debate over the meaning of the Second Amendment is passionate, and it is right that it should be, for the stakes are high. For some people, guns are an evil that should be controlled or eliminated, while others see firearms as essential to every citizen's self-defense and the protection of American democracy.

Any book on the Second Amendment requires a caveat, or warning. Almost all debate over the meaning of the Second Amendment is associated with the battle over gun control in the United States. However, when supporters and opponents of gun control look at the Second Amendment, they take opposite positions on almost everything. They argue over the amendment's background and creation. They disagree on the interpretation of laws and the meaning of court cases about guns. They quarrel about comparisons between the United States and other nations and about the validity of crime statistics. Nor do they agree about the effects of gun control on such basic issues as crime and public safety.

For example, some people believe that crime rates will go down if gun ownership is restricted, while others insist that crime will decrease if everyone owns a gun. Both sides declare with complete certainty that their position is the only correct one and that their opponents are totally mistaken. There is plenty of supporting evidence on both sides: for every innocent five-year-old who accidentally shoots herself with an unwatched handgun, there's a frail ninety-year-old who successfully defends himself by scaring off a burglar breaking into the house.

Therefore, the reader of any book on the Second Amendment must keep in mind that almost every statement on this topic can be and is disputed. This does not mean that nothing at all can be said about the Second Amendment—only that the subject is the source of tremendous controversy.

Gun Use in the United States

It cannot be disputed that guns are involved in many incidents of crime, suicide, and accidents in the United States. In 1998, even though the country was in the middle of a ten-year decline in the homicide rate, more than 30,000 Americans died firearm-related deaths. Of that number, 39 percent were murdered, 57 percent were suicides, 3 percent were accidents, and in 1 percent, the intent was unknown.

Of the 16,765 murders in America in 2000, two-thirds were committed with firearms. For every person murdered with a gun in the United States, there are approximately two injuries that result from firearms use. The role of handguns is particularly noteworthy. In 1996, handguns were used to murder 15 people in Japan, 30 in Great Britain, 106 in Canada, and 9,390 in the United States. In addition, guns sometimes kill people accidentally. In 2000, more than 700 fatal gun accidents were reported in the United States; almost a quarter of the people accidentally killed by guns were under the age of eighteen.

There is no way of accurately knowing exactly how many guns there are in the United States. Estimates range from 60 million to 250 million; 200 million is the number most commonly cited. According to surveys, approximately 40 percent of the families in the United States own some kind of gun and about 25 percent own a handgun. Almost 8 million Americans claim to carry a gun in order to protect themselves. In 1998 alone, licensed

Those who support a person's right to bear arms are as passionate about this right as opponents are about the idea of gun control. These three college students, members of their school's gun club called the Second Amendment Sisters, practice shooting at a range in Springfield, Massachusetts.

firearms dealers sold an estimated 4.4 million guns (1.7 million handguns), but many more were sold illegally.

Guns are widely used in both crime and self-defense. In the United States in 2000, more than 500,000 victims of serious violent crimes such as rape, robbery, and assault stated that they faced an offender who was armed with a gun. Self-defense against crime is also an important reason why people own a gun. Estimates of defensive gun use in the United States range widely from 60,000 to 2.5 million incidents a year.

The Constitution and History

One part of the Second Amendment debate is a historical question. What did the writers of the Constitution actually mean when they wrote that single sentence? Unfortunately, the Constitutional Convention that gathered in Philadelphia, Pennsylvania, in 1787 met in secret, and there are only the sketchiest records of its sessions. Although historians have James Madison to thank for most of the notes that remain, the Constitution was a group effort—the product of many hands and numerous compromises. Many of those present at the convention, such as Madison and Alexander Hamilton, held very different views and changed them frequently, sometimes even during the convention itself, but especially during their political careers. To make matters even more complicated, the Bill of Rights was not a part of the original Constitution, but was proposed mainly by antifederalists—people who opposed the Constitution.

The difficulty in harmonizing these conflicting views explains why it is almost impossible to declare that the Second Amendment (or any part of the Constitution) represents one single or simple original intention. Yet despite these problems, no book on the Second Amendment can avoid at least an attempt to examine the traditions of the British colonists and the assumptions of the writers of the Constitution regarding self-defense, militias, and the right to keep and bear arms.

James Madison, of all the delegates to the Constitutional Convention, kept the most thorough notes of the secret proceedings. With help from his notes, we can make assumptions about the original intent of the Second Amendment and other parts of the Constitution.

Guns in American Culture

More than two centuries have passed since the Constitution was written in 1787. The United States is a far different place in the twenty-first century than it was in the eighteenth. Militias of the type mentioned in the Second Amendment no longer have anything to do with national self-defense, but Americans continue to make, buy, and use guns at one of the highest rates in the world. Americans use these weapons for both legal and illegal purposes: hunting, self-defense, crime, sport, or as collectibles.

As the United States became an urban and suburban nation and as firearms became ever more deadly, people's feelings toward guns have also changed. The decline of the militias, the role of guns in westward expansion, the creation of a professional police force, and violence in American popular culture have all affected and been affected by interpretations of the Second Amendment.

The minuteman, the frontiersman, the cowboy, the gangster, the marine, the police officer, and the drug dealer are all symbols of the United States, spread by mass media throughout the country and the world. All are associated to some degree with the possession of guns and underline the importance of the role of the Second Amendment in American life.

The Modern Debate over the Second Amendment

For more than a century and a half, the Second Amendment played a less controversial role in the United States than most other aspects of the Bill of Rights, such as freedom of speech or the rights of the accused. However, the assassinations of President John F. Kennedy in 1963 and civil rights activist Martin Luther King Jr. and Senator Robert Kennedy in 1968 led to calls for stronger laws regulating guns. At the same time, the emphasis on individual rights that began in that decade led many people to claim that "gun control" laws were an unconstitutional infringement on personal freedom. Since 1968, arguments over the Second Amendment have been commonplace in American politics and law.

Modern laws regarding guns in the United States, such as the Gun Control Act of 1968 and the Brady Handgun Violence Protection Act of 1993, have been among the most bitterly contested in modern American society. The controversy has been fueled by the rise of single-interest advocacy groups such as the National Rifle Association (NRA) and the Brady Campaign to Prevent Gun Violence. For a brief time in the 1980s and 1990s, the theory that the Second Amendment gave Americans the "right to revolution" gained some popularity. This interpretation benefited from violent governmental actions at Waco, Texas, in 1992 and Ruby Ridge, Idaho, in 1993, but lost most of its scholarly support after the terrorist bombing in Oklahoma City in 1995. Since then, debate over the Second Amendment has focused primarily on guns and crime prevention, although the terrorist attack on the United States on September 11, 2001, also has changed the nature of the argument. The modern debate over gun control is a reminder that constitutional questions regarding the Second Amendment are not dry and meaningless exercises in history but debated every day in the media, legislatures, and courts.

The Judicial Question

In America, judges usually decide questions about the meaning of the Constitution. The Supreme Court of the United States possesses the right of judicial review, which means that it can declare both state and federal laws to be in conflict with the Constitution ("unconstitutional") and therefore invalid. Any discussion about the meaning of the Second Amendment and the U.S. Constitution has to refer to these judicial decisions.

The assassinations by gunshot of civil rights leader Martin Luther King Jr. (center), Senator Robert Kennedy, and President John F. Kennedy in the 1960s turned America's attention to the Second Amendment. Martin Luther King Jr. is pictured in Memphis, Tennessee, the day before he was killed.

The beauty of the U.S. Constitution is its flexibility. Because this crucial document is so short, it has been adapted to vastly different time periods. The U.S. Supreme Court has not really issued a broad ruling on the Second Amendment since the case of *United States v. Miller* in 1939. This has allowed an extremely wide range of interpretations to flourish, not just regarding the right to bear arms, but over the very nature of the relationship between the individual states and the federal government. The 2001 decision by a lower federal court that gun ownership is an individual right (in the case of *Emerson v. United States*), and the refusal of the Supreme Court to hear an appeal, ensures that the issue of gun use in America will remain disputed for the foreseeable future.

Yet even if everyone agreed that the Second Amendment gave individuals the right to keep and bear arms for their own private purposes, the debate over gun use in the United States would not end. This is because none of the rights listed in the Bill of Rights is absolute. Governments, whether national, state, or local, have always possessed what is known as "police power." This allows them to take necessary steps to protect the health, safety, and welfare of their citizens, even if those steps conflict with the Bill of Rights. For example, the First Amendment guarantee of freedom of speech is not an acceptable defense against the charge of inciting a riot.

Almost everyone agrees that the government can and should make "reasonable" laws regulating weapons in modern society–otherwise, the neighbors could keep an atomic bomb in their bedroom. At issue, then, is what is "reasonable." In the end, no matter what protections or rights are granted by the Second Amendment, it does not provide the final word on gun use and gun control in the United States. It is, however, the logical place to start a discussion of that subject.

Note: All metric conversions in this book are approximate.

CHAPTER 1

The Right to Bear Arms Before the Constitution

The Second Amendment contains only one sentence, and the meaning of that sentence is disputed. Debates at the Constitutional Convention and in Congress over the issues were short (according to the surviving notes) and do not shed a great deal of light on the correct interpretation. Faced with these difficulties, lawyers and historians often try to understand the Second Amendment by placing it in historical context. To learn about a law and the intentions of its authors, it's often helpful to examine the historical conditions that led to that law.

Common Law, Crime, Self-Defense, and Weapons

FAST FACT

England had no standing army until the 1600s and no regular police force until the 1800s.

The *common law* is the system of justice that began in England and was spread by the British to whatever places they colonized. Common law is based on previous court decisions rather than on specific laws. Common law, therefore, depends on principles that are interpreted by judges rather than rules made by legislators, whether general or specific. If there is no law on a particular subject, such as when one is permitted to kill someone in self-defense, the decisions made by judges become the common law for that subject.

Both British and American common law agreed that people charged with a crime could plead "self-defense." This meant that people were allowed to protect themselves, their families, and, to a lesser degree, their private property when somebody else tried to harm them. A judge (or jury) would decide if the act of self-defense was performed in a legitimate way. Some would argue that the right to own guns began in this common-law right of self-defense.

In England in the early Middle Ages, there was no effective police, and individual citizens were forced to protect themselves and preserve public order. According to common law, when a crime was committed, citizens had to alert their neighbors. Everyone was then expected to pursue the alleged lawbreakers. Villagers who refused to get involved could be fined and imprisoned. In a serious emergency, all able-bodied men between the ages of sixteen and sixty could be called up to serve on a sheriff's posse, chasing criminals or putting down local riots.

Beginning in the late Middle Ages, English monarchs (and Parliament, the British lawmaking body) expected citizens to have the right kinds of weapons to perform these duties. At the same time, the English kings and queens, fearful of revolt and social disorder, sponsored or proclaimed laws restricting the type of weapons that English citizens could own and the ways that they could be used. Later, some game laws restricted gun possession by limiting hunting to people with a certain amount of money or land.

The Militia

A *militia* is a military organization made up of people who are not professional soldiers. In a national emergency, a militia acquired soldiers through either enlistment (of volunteers) or conscription (of draftees). *Conscription* is a

This illustration depicts the Battle of Hastings in 1066, in which the king of England, Harold II, attempted to defend the throne against invaders from Normandy (now part of France). England had no full-time army at this time, but depended on militias consisting of armed citizens.

government's policy of forcing people to serve in its armed forces; a *draftee* is a person who has been drafted, or made to serve in the military by conscription. The militiaman—historically, the militia did not include women—left his civilian duties and became a soldier until the emergency was over. Then he returned to his home and his civilian status.

The first real example of a militia as a defensive organization against invaders was probably the *fyrd*, which was used by the Anglo-Saxons in England before they were conquered by the French from Normandy in 1066. Under Saxon law, from perhaps as early as the 600s, every free man had to join the army, and landowners were supposed to keep a supply of armor and weapons.

Militias were important throughout the Middle Ages, especially in England and the areas now known as Italy and Germany. Famous English militia laws, such as Henry II's Assize of Arms in 1181 and Edward I's Statute of Winchester in 1285, made English subjects responsible, according to their wealth and status, for using arms against crime and in defense of the community and the nation.

The English Civil War (1642–1648) marked the beginning of a turbulent time in the history of Britain. King Charles I, shown here in battle, was executed as a result of the war. In the decades of change that followed, the issue of who in Britain should and should not be allowed to own weapons came to the forefront.

By the late 1500s, the rise of large professional armies in Europe led to the gradual decline in the use of militias. In the years ahead, as North America was colonized, militias would regain their importance there, where there were no large armies.

The English Civil War and Its Aftermath

In the mid-1600s, there was a series of dramatic political events during and following the English Civil War (1642–1648). One constant characteristic of this period was a great deal of quarreling in Great Britain between Catholics and Protestants, two competing branches of the Christian religion. Although most people in Britain had switched from Catholicism to Protestantism in the 1500s, many still remained Catholics.

FAST FACT

In 1642, the first year of the English Civil War, Parliament passed a law that allowed officers of the government to enter the homes of Catholics and other supporters of royalty in order to take away their weapons, horses, and ammunition.

From 1649 to 1658, Protestant leader Oliver Cromwell ruled England. Under Cromwell's dictatorship, King Charles I was executed and Catholics were persecuted. Cromwell's rule was originally popular, but it depended so much on his personal character that it collapsed almost immediately after his death.

Only two years after Cromwell's death, the English welcomed Charles II (son of Charles I) back to assume the British throne. He ruled until his death in 1685, when his brother, James II, succeeded him. Charles II was very sympathetic to Catholicism (he died a Catholic) and James II converted to that religion in 1668. Both kings took the divine right of kings very seriously and tried to rule like dictators. (The *divine right of kings* was the belief that a king's right to rule comes directly from God and not from the people.) This put them on a collision course with Parliament, at that time composed of the English nobility, owners of country estates, merchants, and some artisans.

Under Charles II, Parliament banned all but wealthy landowners from owning firearms. In 1670 and 1671, it prohibited the keeping of guns and bows by all persons who didn't possess lands or leases that produced at least £100 in annual rent. People who qualified to own weapons

FAST FACT

The unpopular, dictatorial, and Catholic King James II had few loyal followers in England. The English, who did not want to execute another king as they had Charles I, allowed James to escape to France, where he died in 1701.

were given the power to search the houses of their tenants and to take any firearms that they found there.

In a complete reversal from the extreme Protestantism of the Cromwell years, James II now attempted to turn Great Britain into a Catholic nation. The king appointed Catholics to top government posts and increased the size of the standing army. James II even attempted to disarm Protestants in England, although the nation had a majority Protestant population.

The birth of James II's son in 1688, who would have succeeded him instead of James II's daughter, the Protestant Mary, and her husband, William of Orange, united all the king's opponents. Parliament peacefully engineered the overthrow of James II and replaced him with William and Mary in an event known as the Glorious Revolution of 1688.

The British Bill of Rights and the Right to Bear Arms

FAST FACT

The British Bill of Rights stated that no Catholic could ever again become king or queen of England.

In 1689, the year after the Glorious Revolution, Parliament adopted the British Bill of Rights (also known as the Declaration of Rights). The British Bill of Rights listed a series of specific complaints against James II and then declared that these actions were illegal. More importantly, it stated that English subjects possessed certain civil and political rights that were inalienable—that is, they were fundamental rights that could not be taken away. The British Bill of Rights also placed the power of Parliament over that of the monarchy in Britain. The document remains one of the most important milestones in the history of law and political freedom.

In Article VII, the British Bill of Rights states "that the Subjects which are Protestants, may have Arms for their Defense suitable to their Condition, and as allowed by law." This provision of the British Bill of Rights is often cited as the forerunner of the Second Amendment in the U.S. Bill of Rights.

How Relevant Is Article VII?

According to one interpretation, the reference to the "law" that qualifies Article VII in the British Bill of Rights referred to the 1671 law that firearms could be owned only by the nobility, wealthy landowners, and members of the militia defending the country. In this view, Article VII was not meant to address the long-accepted right of the government to regulate the possession of arms but rather the question of who had that right—the king or Parliament. Article VII hardly grants a universal right to arms; instead it qualifies this right by religion ("which are Protestants"), status or wealth ("suitable to their Condition"), and parliamentary restriction ("as allowed by law").

An alternative reading of the ambiguous wording, however, leaves open the possibility that the reference is to the common law. In this case, individuals would have the right to "have Arms for their Defense" under any circumstances, and no law could take this right away.

Some historians have argued that Article VII of the British Bill of Rights changed the medieval English

King James II (center, seated) looks distressed in this illustration that depicts the moment when he read that his daughter, Mary, and her husband, William of Orange, had come to England from the Netherlands to take over the throne. James II was Catholic, and William and Mary were Protestants.

obligation of able-bodied men to serve in the militia into an individual right to keep and bear arms (although that particular phrasing is not used in the document). Others claim that the right of the individual Englishman to have arms was always restricted.

The surviving record of the debates and other documents relating to the U.S. Bill of Rights never directly refers to Article VII at all. The British Bill of Rights was crucial to the political worldview of the colonists, and almost all educated Americans in the late 1700s were familiar with it. However, the absence of the British Bill of Rights in discussions and debates over the American Second Amendment, and the fact that its wording is rather different from that of the Constitution, greatly limits the usefulness of the English tradition in helping to interpret the Second Amendment.

Colonial America and Guns

White settlers in America in the 1600s depended on their own skills to protect themselves against wild animals, hostile Native Americans, and marauding foreign soldiers. Anyone who could use a weapon, usually excluding blacks and women, had to help out in local defense. Colonial governments did not have enough money to arm their citizens, so from the earliest days of the British colonies in America, able-bodied men had to not only serve in the militia but provide their own arms and ammunition.

Colonial America was primarily rural; in the 1790 census, only 5 percent of Americans lived in cities with a population over 2,500. Hunting provided food for both Native Americans and the Europeans who invaded the continent in the 1600s and 1700s, although its importance and popularity are disputed. Hunting could also generate extra income for some farm families. Competitive sport shooting was a popular form of recreation dating back to colonial times. These matches glorified marksmanship, which had at least some relationship to the ability to survive in rural America.

The Colonial Fear of a Standing Army

The British colonists in America were often at war, to a greater or lesser degree, with the French, the Spanish, or Native Americans. The most effective protection against these threats was a professional army. Colonial Americans, however, were deeply suspicious of what they called a "standing army." Throughout European history, professional soldiers had overthrown civilian governments and taken away the rights and liberties of the people. In the Renaissance, from the fourteenth to the sixteenth century, famous writers such as Desiderius Erasmus, Thomas More, and Niccolò Machiavelli made fun of war and favored the concept of civilian defense. Many educated men in America knew these writings. American colonial thinkers were also deeply influenced by British political philosophers known as the Radical Whigs. These men emphasized small, decentralized government and the dangers to liberty posed by a peacetime army.

Gun ownership during colonial times in America was an important component of everyday life. Hunting, as shown in this painting from the 1800s, was one way that colonists and Native Americans got food. Citizens also had to be armed in order to defend their colony.

John Trenchard and Thomas Gordon were two of the best-known Radical Whigs. In 1721 and 1722, they jointly published a series of essays in Great Britain known as *Cato's Letters*. Trenchard and Gordon warned that the people must always be on guard to restrain royal power. The attacks on the existence of standing armies in *Cato's Letters* deeply influenced generations of American thinkers, including John Adams and Thomas Jefferson.

The Militia in America

The Military Company of Massachusetts (later known as the Ancient and Honorable Artillery Company) was chartered by the Massachusetts Bay Colony in 1637. The charter proclaimed the basic right and duty of each citizen to defend those whom he loved and the belief that only through properly organized training could Massachusetts men perform this crucial service. Governor John Winthrop refused to approve the charter for more than a year, fearing the possibility of military influence on the civil government. Increasing problems with Native Americans

When a young George Washington (on horseback) went into battle against the French in the French and Indian War (1754–1763), he brought militia fighters from Virginia with him. An organized army would have made a better fighting force, but there was none in the colonies at that time.

made him change his mind, however, and he signed the charter on March 13, 1638. This was the first organized militia in a British colony in North America.

Other American colonies formed organizations similar to the Massachusetts militia. These militias were usually made up of adult white males of fighting age (roughly between eighteen and forty-five). The colonial governments required these men to enroll for military service. They received limited training, served for a brief time (from a few days to a few weeks), and were usually under local command. Americans preferred this system to the concept of paid professional soldiers, who were usually volunteers, enlisted for several years, received a great deal of military training, served even in peacetime, and would have been under national control. Many American politicians and political writers glorified the militia, representing the people as a whole as the very essence of democracy. The ideal of the militia linked two essential elements of the American colonial worldview: local control and voluntary service.

The citizen's obligation to serve in the militia resulted in a good deal of regulation of firearms ownership in colonial America. Since the colonies and local governments did not provide the weaponry, laws often required all eligible males to own guns to support the local militia. Other regulations, however, barred various groups from owning guns and serving in the militia. Depending on the colony, this might mean Catholics, indentured servants, or free or enslaved African-Americans. Women might know how to handle guns, and even be state citizens, but they were never considered to be eligible for the militia.

The British Army in America

The British victory over the French in the French and Indian War (1754–1763) gave the British control over eastern North America, but Great Britain's national debt had nearly doubled as a result of the war. Money was needed to pay this debt. Since taxes were already far higher in Britain than in

America, Parliament thought that it was only fair to raise taxes on imports to and exports from the American colonies, arguing that the war had been fought on their behalf.

The British also needed to raise money to support the troops now stationed in the newly conquered province of Canada. At the end of the war, a British peacetime army of 10,000 men was placed in North America to intimidate the Native Americans on the frontier, the French in Quebec, and the Spanish in Florida. The presence of this army also displayed the willingness of the British to use military force to preserve their authority in the colonies.

Until 1763, Britain had ruled America indirectly; now British officials controlled American taxation, legal proceedings, and military finances. Suddenly, many

The presence of the English army in the colonies after the French and Indian War was just one of the factors that led to the colonists' growing displeasure at being governed from afar by England. In this scene from Boston in 1765, for example, colonists burn documents in protest against the stamp tax.

Americans were reminded, to their shock, that they were, in fact, residents of colonies of England. New British policies threatened their traditional local power and authority.

For example, in September 1768, colonists held a meeting, led by James Otis, Samuel Adams, John Hancock, and Samuel Cushing, in Faneuil Hall in Boston, Massachusetts. These men protested the new British policies, especially the Townshend Acts of 1767 and the peacetime professional army in the colonies. They passed a resolution reminding the British that Protestants had been permitted arms during the reign of William and Mary. Therefore, they declared, the British should supply every soldier and housekeeper in Massachusetts with a musket and ammunition in accordance with the law. In February 1769, Parliament declared that these proceedings in Boston were illegal and were really aimed at inciting treason and revolution.

Trouble in Massachusetts

British taxes on trade goods struck the merchants of Boston, as well as the rest of the population that depended on their prosperity, in their pocketbooks. Several riots took place in Massachusetts as a result, including one that forced British officials to flee to a British ship for safety. The British decided to take a hard line; by the end of 1768, over 1,000 British soldiers were encamped in Boston, and 4,000 were there by 1770 in a town of only 15,000 people.

In March 1770, a patrol of British soldiers, taunted by a mob of laborers and sailors, fired into the crowd and killed five men. Although a local jury acquitted the soldiers, James Bowdoin's widely circulated pamphlet depicted the incident as a "Boston Massacre." This greatly increased American resentment of and opposition to standing armies. Colonists feared that their liberties, guaranteed by the English Bill of Rights, were fading away. Without representation in Parliament, or even a legal way to negotiate, some colonists began to speak about armed revolution.

Lexington and Concord

In 1774, Massachusetts residents once again organized armed resistance to British measures. In August, 150 delegates from nearby towns met in Concord for the Middlesex County Congress. This convention (illegal, from the British point of view) advised Americans to stop supporting the British colonial government. Armed crowds began to harass colonial officials and prevented judges appointed by the British governor from holding court. The Massachusetts House of Representatives, outlawed by Britain's Coercive Acts of that year, met illegally and functioned as an alternative government, collecting taxes, passing laws, and organizing armed militias.

General Thomas Gage, the military governor of Massachusetts, tried desperately to maintain British power. In September 1774, he ordered British troops to march out of Boston and capture American weapons and supplies at Charlestown and Cambridge, Massachusetts. Although he succeeded in raiding local gunpowder and artillery supplies, Gage was shocked when almost 10,000 colonial militiamen, responding to false rumors of bloodshed, belatedly mobilized to protect the military depots in Concord and Worcester. The Concord town meeting voted to raise a military force of armed citizens—the famous minutemen—to "stand at a minute's warning in case of alarm." Neighboring Massachusetts towns also prepared their militias for rapid action.

For six months, Gage would not risk another expedition into the Massachusetts countryside that might lead to an armed conflict and ruin all possibility of compromise between the British and the Americans. However, in April 1775, Lord Dartmouth, the British colonial secretary, proclaimed Massachusetts to be in a state of open rebellion and ordered Gage to strike quickly at the Americans.

On the night of April 18, Gage sent 700 soldiers to capture colonial leaders, supplies, and weapons at Concord. The Americans were warned, and at dawn the next day, local

The so-called Boston Massacre of 1770 made Americans more distrustful of a standing army than ever before. British soldiers stationed in the city fired into a crowd of citizens that had been taunting them, killing five. The soldiers were not found guilty of any crime, but public opinion was already formed against them.

militiamen met the British on the village green at Lexington. No one knows who fired first, but shots rang out, and a British volley killed eight Americans. The British then marched to Concord but were unsuccessful in their mission. When they tried to retreat along the narrow, winding roads to Boston (now the route of the Boston Marathon), they were repeatedly ambushed by 1,000 militiamen from neighboring towns. By the end of the day, 73 British soldiers had been killed and 174 wounded; American casualties were 49 dead and 39 wounded. The American Revolution (1775–1783) had begun.

The Cincinnatus Complex

In his official report to General Gage only days after the battle, a British officer, Franklin Smith, commented on the effectiveness of the American militia. He wrote, "I can't think but it must have been a preconcerted scheme in them, to attack the King's troops the first favorable

The first battle of the Revolutionary War, at Lexington, Massachusetts, began when local militia met British troops on the village green. The British were on their way to neighboring Concord to seize weapons and other supplies, and the Americans, warned of their plan, were there to stop them.

opportunity that offered; otherwise, I think they could not, in such a short a time from our marching out, have raised such a numerous body."

The embattled Massachusetts farmers who resisted the British advance were well trained. By fighting so effectively, they spread the idea that the militiamen could defeat any professional soldiers. This glorification of the citizen militia is sometimes known as "the Cincinnatus complex," after an ancient Roman soldier. The memory of these valiant militiamen would play a crucial role in the later debates over the role of a professional army in America and the phrasing of the Second Amendment to the Constitution.

The Declaration of Independence

The presence of British troops in America angered colonists more than any issue other than Parliamentary taxation. In 1776, Samuel Adams wrote that a "standing army, however necessary it may be at some times, is always dangerous to the liberties of the people." Even George Washington, who was notoriously distrustful of the use of militias, observed that professional armies "have at one time or another subverted the liberties of almost all the Countries they have been raised to defend." The Virginia Bill of Rights, written in 1776, declared that "standing armies, in time of peace, should be avoided, as dangerous liberty." Other states copied Virginia's wording. Four states—Pennsylvania, North Carolina, Vermont, and Massachusetts—included some form of the right to bear arms in their formal declarations of rights.

The Declaration of Independence, signed in Philadelphia on July 4, 1776, reflected this hostility toward a professional army. The Declaration specifically complained that George III, the king of England, "has kept among us, in Times of Peace, Standing Armies, without the consent of our legislatures. He has affected to render the Military independent of and superior to the Civil Power." The Declaration also criticized the British for "quartering large Bodies of Armed Troops among us [and] protecting them, by a mock trial, from punishment for any Murders which they should commit on the Inhabitants of these states."

FAST FACT

Cincinnatus was a legendary ancient Roman leader who came from his farm to defend Rome and then returned to his farm after the city was saved. Educated eighteenth-century Americans who had a love of classical history often compared his career to George Washington's.

The Natural Rights Tradition and the Right to Bear Arms

The signers of the Declaration of Independence were greatly influenced by what is known as the "natural rights tradition." Part of this tradition idealized the citizen-soldier as the best way to make sure that rights were protected in a republic. Niccolò Machiavelli, the Renaissance writer, especially related bearing arms to what he called "civic virtue." He believed that weapons were essential for the individual citizen to protect himself, defend his state, and to ensure that rulers listened to the people (all citizens were male to Machiavelli). In Book I of *The Art of War,* from 1521, Machiavelli attacked a peacetime army and glorified a militia; a state, he claimed, "should

FAST FACT

In *The Prince,* Machiavelli famously stated,

The chief foundations of all states, new as well as old or composite, are good laws and good arms; and as there cannot be good laws where the state is not well armed, it follows that where they are well armed they have good laws.... Among other evils which being unarmed brings you, it causes you to be despised.

employ its own citizens in times of war and subsequently dismiss them to pursue their former occupation."

Although the seventeenth-century English philosopher John Locke never specifically mentioned a right to bear arms for personal self-defense, he clearly felt that people had the right to do whatever was necessary to protect their natural right to life, liberty, and property. By extension, this gave the people the right—indeed, the obligation—to resist oppression when rulers become tyrannical. The Declaration of Independence expressed Locke's idea by stating that "all men are created equal, that they are endowed by their Creator with certain unalienable rights, that among these are Life, Liberty, and the pursuit of Happiness. That to secure these rights, Governments are instituted among Men, deriving their just powers from the consent of the governed."

Niccolò Machiavelli (1469–1527) believed not only that weapons were important to a strong society, but that its "good laws" depended upon "good arms" to uphold them. The signers of the Declaration of Independence were greatly influenced by the writings of Machiavelli and others.

Two conflicting conclusions can be drawn from this statement of natural rights. It seems that all men have an inalienable right to defend themselves against violence, not just by other people, but also against tyranny and oppression by the government itself. No one, however, could effectively exercise this right without weapons. Therefore, Americans—and indeed, all people—possess a natural right to own guns.

On the other hand, while people living in a wild state have the right to use force for self-defense, that right might not be inalienable. According to British philosopher Thomas Hobbes, it was the very use of force that made life in a natural state one of "continual fear and danger of violent death; and the life of man, solitary, poor, nasty, brutish, and short." Instead, as French philosopher Jean-Jacques Rousseau observed, individuals establish governments with the consent of the governed. A sort of exchange then takes place; people give up some of their right to violent self-defense as long as the government can establish and maintain public order under the rule of law.

The American Revolution

In the American Revolution, Americans fought the British with a combination of a professional army and the militia. The Continental Army served as the main fighting force, aided by various state militias. In the crucial Saratoga, New York, campaign in 1777, the militias played a key role in winning the battle. Citizen-soldiers with their Pennsylvania rifles, serving in state-based militias, helped win the American Revolution against the finest standing army in the world.

Yet although militias provided valuable service in the American Revolution, their flaws did not go unnoticed. Many units lacked discipline and training, and militia soldiers could not be relied on to serve long periods of time. At Camden, South Carolina, many militiamen panicked and fled without firing a shot, handing the

FAST FACT

During the American Revolution, the individual colonies (and then states) had a variety of laws regarding gun ownership. Several governments kept the right to order their residents to hand in their firearms if they were needed for military purposes. In order to do this, the government had the power to conduct gun censuses—that is, to count, locate, and note the condition of guns owned throughout the colony.

British control of the colony in 1780. General George Washington, commander in chief of the Continental Army, defended the militias in public. In private, however, he wrote the Continental Congress, "To place any dependence upon Militia, is, assuredly, resting upon a broken staff...."

The Situation at the End of the American Revolution

The Treaty of Paris in 1783 ended hostilities between the American colonists and Great Britain. The treaty officially acknowledged the independence of the United States and defined its western boundary at the Mississippi River.

The signers of the Declaration of Independence had a tremendous fear of *anarchy* (social and political disorder). Although they were revolutionaries who used violence to overthrow the British government, they wrote the Declaration specifically because they wanted the "decent respect [of] the opinions of mankind." To get it, they assured the world that their new nation would not lack a government. According to Thomas Jefferson, it was the right and duty of a free people to alter or abolish a despotic government but then "to institute new Government, laying its foundations on such principles and organizing its powers in such form, as to them shall seem most likely to effect their Safety and Happiness."

In 1776, no one was sure what this new government would look like, who would participate in it, or how much power it would have. These were all questions that would have to be resolved in the critical years when the Constitution and the Bill of Rights were written.

CHAPTER 2

The Creation of the Second Amendment

FAST FACT

Militia members traditionally owned their own weapons, a policy that dated from medieval England and spread with the colonists to America. Article VI of the Articles of Confederation, however, represented a newer view that arming the militia was a public responsibility of the government.

The first government of the newly independent American states was organized under the Articles of Confederation. The Continental Congress sent this plan to the states in the middle of the American Revolution in November 1777, but it was not fully *ratified,* or approved, until 1781. The Articles of Confederation created a loose confederation of almost independent states. The authors intentionally created a weak national government, with no national supreme court or president. The Declaration of Independence had claimed that Great Britain's government was too powerful and too far away; Americans tried to avoid similar problems when they formed their first government by making it relatively weak.

The Articles of Confederation also reflected the American suspicion of standing armies by giving the main job of national defense to the states. The Articles specifically stated in Article VI that "every State shall always keep up a well regulated and disciplined militia, sufficiently armed and accoutered [equipped], and shall provide and constantly have ready for use, in public stores, a due number of field pieces [large weapons such as cannons] and tents, and a proper quantity of arms, ammunition and camp equipage." Article IX stated that the congress's military powers could be exercised only by a vote of nine of thirteen states. Nothing at all was said about a national standing army.

The years after the Treaty of Paris officially gave America its independence were often difficult, especially in the realm of foreign affairs. Native Americans inflicted several defeats on the militia on the frontier, Spain disputed the southern boundary of the United States and threatened to restrict access to the Mississippi River, and the British refused to evacuate their forts in the northwest. As a result, some Americans began to rethink the Articles of Confederation and consider the need for a stronger central government.

The Writing of the Constitution

Shays's Rebellion was an uprising by farmers in western Massachusetts in 1786 and 1787. They were protesting

Militiamen from eastern Massachusetts fire on a rebellious mob led by farmer Daniel Shays in the western part of the state in 1787. Shays's Rebellion made those in power, revolutionaries themselves, realize that their new government needed to be made stronger.

high taxes and the seizing of farms for unpaid debts. This revolt horrified the now cautious men who ran the American government. It was one thing to rebel against a government that did not allow representation to citizens, but quite another to rebel when the legally elected government was now made up of the old revolutionaries. Shays's Rebellion was crushed by militia companies from eastern Massachusetts in 1787. Afterward, many American political thinkers agreed that it was time to create a stronger national government.

In the summer of 1787, nationalists gathered in Philadelphia to make some changes to the Articles of Confederation. Instead, they wrote an entirely new document known as the Constitution, which remains the supreme law of the United States to this day; no other law can contradict it.

Everyone realized that if the Constitution was going to work, states could not override national laws. The opening phrase of Article VI of the Constitution is sometimes known as the "supremacy clause"; it clearly states, "This Constitution, and the laws of the United States which shall be made in pursuance thereof; and all treaties made, or which shall be made, under the authority of the United States, shall be the supreme law of the land."

Nonetheless, the new Constitution established a "federal system" based on dividing up the powers of government between the nation and the states. This meant that the individual states would keep a good deal of their old authority and many of their traditional rights. Americans of the time tended to view themselves as citizens of their states first and of the nation second—an attitude that would last until the end of the American Civil War (1861–1865). The federal system in the Constitution checked the power of this new, stronger central government.

The Constitution and the Militia

After the experience of Shays's Rebellion, conservatives wanted the new federal government to have the necessary power to enforce its laws and defend itself. However, the authors of the Constitution, now referred to as its "framers," knew that Americans did not trust standing armies and that this fear had led to the Revolution. In the Constitutional debates, James Madison noted that "as the greatest danger to liberty is from large standing armies, it is best to prevent them by an effectual provision for a good Militia." So the writers of the Constitution compromised; the new Constitution recognized both the militia and a standing army.

Article I, Section 8, of the Constitution gave the U.S. Congress the power to "raise and support armies," "provide and maintain a navy," and to finance and regulate both. The national Congress would also have authority over the state militias; it could "provide for calling forth the Militia" in order to "execute the Laws of the Union, suppress Insurrections and repel invasions."

The Constitution also assigned Congress the power to "provide for organizing, arming, and disciplining, the

Militia, and for governing such Part of them as may be employed in the Service of the United States." Rather than declare that militias in the future would have to be identical to the way they were in 1787, Article I, Section 8, said that a militia could take whatever form Congress desired.

In Article II, Section 2, the president was appointed "commander in chief of the army and navy of the United States, and of the militia of the several States, when called into the actual service of the United States." This seemed to give the national government (through the president) considerable control over the local militias.

On the other hand, the Constitution granted the individual states some control over their militias. Article I, Section 8, reserved "to the States respectively, the Appointment of the Officers, and the Authority of training the Militia according to the discipline prescribed by Congress." However, even the last part of this sentence allowed Congress to intrude on militia organization.

The Debate Between Federalists and Antifederalists

The people who opposed the Constitution were known as *antifederalists.* This group contained some of the most famous supporters of the American Revolution: Patrick Henry, Samuel Adams, George Mason, and Elbridge Gerry. They worried a great deal about the power of this new central government created by the Constitution. Antifederalists believed that the government that was closest to the people was the best government. They feared that the Constitution's design, even with its checks and balances and division of powers, would still not be enough to safeguard liberty. The antifederalists insisted on a Bill of Rights to protect the people against the national government. One of their constant demands was that the individual states should continue to control their own militias.

Samuel Adams was a leader of the antifederalists, or those opposed to the Constitution. Fearing a strong central government, they favored instead state governments that were closer to and more aware of the needs of their people. One antifederalist concern was maintaining the states' control over their own militias.

On the other hand, federalists such as Alexander Hamilton, James Madison, John Adams, and John Jay believed that America would never fulfill its commercial potential—or worse, it might drift into anarchy—without a stronger central government. They thought that a powerful national government could be controlled through the checks and balances that were written into the Constitution. Antifederalists feared the domination of a national government by the wealthy and the powerful, but federalists worried about the so-called "tyranny of the majority"—mobs that would take away other people's rights and liberties, especially the right to property. This debate between federalists and antifederalists over peoples' rights led directly to the adoption of the Bill of Rights.

The Federalist Papers

Defenders of the Constitution tried to counter the charges of the antifederalists that the new Constitution would lead to dictatorship. Probably the most famous effort was a series of essays, now known as *The Federalist Papers,* published in 1787 and 1788. These were written by Alexander Hamilton, James Madison, and John Jay to influence the ratification debate in the state of New York. Although the essays were not widely read or cited in the 1800s, they have become a classic work of political theory and important in current arguments over the meaning of the Constitution.

Hamilton, an outspoken supporter of a very strong central government, tried to drum up support for a standing army and federal control of the militias. He argued that a professional army was naturally superior on the battlefield and quicker to respond in case of emergency. He also claimed that the national government must have the power to impose "uniformity in the organization and discipline" of the militias in order to make them efficient. Hamilton admitted that most Americans' first allegiance was to their home states. He feared, however, that strong state militias would eventually undermine the Constitution and break apart the Union.

James Madison also wanted the Constitution ratified by New York, but he argued in a contradictory fashion from Hamilton. Madison praised the virtues of the state militias and denied the charges of antifederalists that a standing national army would one day lead to the downfall of state governments. Madison calculated that the militias would always have a numerical advantage over any American army and would be able to defeat them in battle. In state militias, Madison claimed, armed male citizens would choose their own officers, fight for their common liberties, and willingly support the government that represented them.

FAST FACT

James Madison would later be the fourth president of the United States, from 1809 to 1817, and lead the United States into the War of 1812 (1812–1815) against the British. Despite Madison's faith in citizen-soldiers, the militias performed so badly in the War of 1812 that they caused several military disasters and almost lost the war.

The Ratification of the Constitution

The ratification of the Constitution was always in doubt in highly populated and economically powerful states such as Massachusetts, Virginia, and New York. These states were naturally reluctant to give up some of their power to the new national government. In order to win

George Washington, who served as president of the Constitutional Convention, oversees the signing of the Constitution in Philadelphia in September 1787. The document, now approved by the convention, then had to go to the individual states for their approval, or ratification.

over these states, leading federalists finally promised their opponents that they would amend the Constitution with a Bill of Rights as soon as possible if only the antifederalists would support the new government. This promise addressed a powerful antifederalist objection to the Constitution, and the document was narrowly ratified at conventions in Massachusetts (187 to 168), Virginia (89 to 79), and New York (30 to 27) in 1788.

The Constitution laid out a framework for the government of the United States. Although it did list several protections against the power of the national government, it was drafted, signed, sent to the states, and ratified without a Bill of Rights.

The Bill of Rights and State Power

The Constitution created a new national legislature to make laws. It was made up of two parts: the House of Representatives and the Senate. True to his word, James Madison, now a member of the House of Representatives from Virginia, introduced nineteen possible constitutional amendments on June 7, 1789. Madison, who had originally argued that a Bill of Rights was unnecessary, based his amendments on the rights guaranteed in various state constitutions and also on a series of proposals by the state conventions that had ratified the Constitution. Congress approved twelve of these amendments, and ten were ratified by the states by the end of 1791. These ten amendments have become known as the Bill of Rights; ironically, what are now considered fundamental freedoms were then just amendments to the Constitution.

The Bill of Rights protected Americans in federal courts by guaranteeing the rights of the accused, such as a trial by jury and freedom from self-incrimination. (*Self-incrimination* is the giving of evidence or testimony that would likely subject one to prosecution.) The amendments also put certain individual rights, such as freedom of speech and religion, directly into the Constitution. The Tenth Amendment forbade the national government from claiming powers that the Constitution did not give it; these unnamed powers were "reserved to the States respectively, or to the people."

The Bill of Rights was created to restrict the powers of the national government. For example, the First Amendment specifically protects the freedoms of speech, press, assembly, religion, and petition only against those laws made by the national Congress. The actions of individual states are controlled only by state laws and state constitutions. If South Carolina wanted to restrict the freedoms of its free black residents, that was the state's business alone. This would become a crucial issue in later interpretations of the Second Amendment.

The authors of the Bill of Rights assumed that the state governments, located nearer to the people that they served, were less likely to oppress Americans. Political thinkers of the day rarely considered that individual freedoms might need national protection against state invasions of the rights of the people (such as in the case of blacks in the South). In 1833, the U.S. Supreme Court confirmed this idea in the case of *Barron v. Baltimore;* the Court ruled that the Bill of Rights only protected citizens from abuses by the national government and not the states. This situation did not begin to change until the ratification of the Fourteenth Amendment in 1868, and only in the twentieth century did federal courts begin to use the Fourteenth Amendment to apply the Bill of Rights to actions by the state. The degree to which the states have to follow the Bill of Rights, however, is still open to dispute, especially in regard to the Second Amendment.

The Second Amendment, the Militias, and the Antifederalists

The Constitution created a national standing army and gave the federal government vast new power over the state militias. Antifederalists were extremely worried that this power would be used not only to weaken the state militias (if the government refused to organize, arm, or train them) but to destroy state authority completely and, with it, individual freedom.

This issue was especially important to citizens of the large and crucial state of Virginia, which counted more slaves than any other state at the time. Patrick Henry, revolutionary and antifederalist, asked at the Virginia ratifying convention, "Have we [in Virginia] the means of resisting disciplined armies, when our only defense, the militia, is put into the hands of Congress?" Henry worried that the state militia would not be sufficiently armed: "The great object is, that every man be armed. But can the people afford to pay for double sets of arms, &c.?"

George Mason had worked on the Constitution as a delegate but then refused to sign it. Back home, he pressed the Virginia convention to obtain "an express declaration, that the State Governments might arm and discipline the militia should Congress fail to do so." This type of antifederalist reasoning struck a chord with the Virginia convention, and the delegates suggested additional wording to the Constitution when Virginia ratified the document. Contained within this statement were at least four different lines of thought:

> That the people have a right to keep and bear arms; that a well regulated Militia...is the proper, natural, and safe defense of a free State. That standing armies in time of peace are dangerous to liberty, and therefore ought to be avoided, as far as circumstances and protection of the Community will admit; and that in all cases the military should be under strict subordination to and governed by the Civil power.

All these ideas would play a role in the shaping of the Second Amendment, although their exact relationship to each other (such as which, if any, is most important) is unclear.

Following Virginia's lead, New Hampshire, New York, North Carolina, and Rhode Island adopted similar

Luther Martin (1744–1826) was a delegate to the Constitutional Convention, but refused to sign the document. He felt that if the federal government continued to control the states' militias, the states would eventually cease to exist. He was not the only delegate with this view.

resolutions. In the Southern states, whites wanted to make sure that they could depend on adequately armed state militias to prevent enslaved African-Americans from revolting. Slave owners feared that a national government dominated by Northerners and commercial interests would destroy the slavery system by disarming the militia, on which plantation owners depended to keep blacks (one-third of the Southern population) in chains. Slave owners now supported an amendment guaranteeing the right of the people to keep and bear arms within the state militia.

At the Pennsylvania ratifying convention, Robert Whitehill attempted to prevent the ratification of the Constitution by offering fifteen proposals to the convention on the day scheduled for a final vote. One of these delaying motions suggested in a catchall fashion:

> That the people have a right to bear arms for the purpose of defense of themselves and their own State, or the United States, or for the purpose of killing game, and no law shall be passed for disarming the people of any of them, unless for crimes committed, or real danger of public injury from individuals; and as standing armies in time of peace are dangerous to liberty, they ought not to be kept up; and that the military shall be kept under strict subordination to and be governed by the civil power.

The convention did not treat seriously Whitehill's mention of "killing game" and "disarming the people," and the amendment was defeated. This type of phrasing did not appear in the debates over the Second Amendment, and neither James Madison nor any antifederalists in Congress proposed amendments along these lines.

State Bills of Rights

The Second Amendment was not the first reference to a right to bear arms. There were similar provisions in the state constitutions of Pennsylvania, North Carolina, Vermont, and Massachusetts. On one hand, these state Bills of Rights seem to limit state powers and therefore give an individual a right to private ownership of arms. On the other hand, some state Bills of Rights draw a clear distinction between the rights of every "individual" (or "man") and the rights of "the people." In these cases, the right to bear arms is always listed as a right of the people as a whole. The dispute over the meaning of these declarations is not unimportant. Madison and those who ratified the Second Amendment might have understood it as meaning something slightly different from similar provisions in these state Bills of Rights, but it seems

The Bill of Rights, which guaranteed certain rights to citizens, was added to the Constitution in 1791. It was originally intended to restrict the federal government only, giving the states freedom to determine their own rules regarding these rights. This issue is still debated today, especially as it applies to the Second Amendment.

Congress of the United States
begun and held at the City of New-York, on
Wednesday the fourth of March, one thousand seven hundred and eighty nine.

THE

RESOLVED

ARTICLES

Article the first.

Article the second.

Article the third.

Article the fourth.

Article the fifth.

Article the sixth.

Article the seventh.

Article the eighth.

Article the ninth.

Article the tenth.

Article the eleventh.

Article the twelfth.

unlikely that they understood it as meaning something extraordinarily different.

In fact, when Madison wrote the suggested amendments to the Constitution that formed the basis of the Bill of Rights, he specifically considered the examples of these state Bills of Rights, as well as hundreds of amendments suggested by the state conventions that ratified the Constitution. Several of the suggested amendments relating to the Second Amendment dealt with how the militia would be trained, when and for how long martial law could be declared, whether a militia could fight beyond the state's borders, and how much military control the state would give up to the national government. (*Martial law* is law administered by military force during an emergency.)

Alternative Wordings of the Second Amendment

Madison preferred a simple style in almost all the amendments that he put before the House of Representatives on June 8, 1789. The first draft of what would become the Second Amendment seemed to deal primarily with military matters, and the emphasis on militias became, if anything, stronger in the final wording. The first draft read:

> The right of the people to keep and bear arms shall not be infringed; a well armed, and well regulated militia being the best security of a free country; but no person religiously scrupulous of bearing arms, shall be compelled to render military service in person.

The phrase "religiously scrupulous" referred to conscientious objectors—people like some Quakers, who did not believe in war and usually would not serve in the army.

In the second draft, as reported on July 28, the section on the militia was moved to the beginning. By reversing the reference to the military and the right of the people to keep and bear arms, this draft seemed to place greater emphasis on the militia. The amendment now read:

> A well regulated militia, composed of the body of the people, being the best security of a free State, the right of the people to keep and bear arms shall not be infringed, but no person religiously scrupulous shall be compelled to bear arms.

The change from "free country" to "free State" seemed to emphasize the importance of a state's separate militias, as opposed to the common defense of the country.

On August 24, the House passed this wording:

> A well regulated militia, composed of the body of the People, being the best security of a free State, the right of the People to keep and bear arms, shall not be infringed, but no one religiously scrupulous of bearing arms, shall be compelled to render military service in person.

This version went to the Senate, where the last part was dropped, perhaps for the sake of brevity or perhaps due to disagreement with its content. In its final form, the Second Amendment now read:

> A well regulated militia, being necessary to the security of a free State, the right of the people to keep and bear arms, shall not be infringed.

Things certainly would have been simpler if the Second Amendment had mimicked the wording of the First Amendment and read, "Congress shall make no law infringing on the right of the people to keep and bear arms." The peculiarity of the actual phrasing as ratified leaves considerable room for interpretation. Whether the first part ("A well regulated militia...") is a clarification of the second clause ("the right of the people..."), equal to it, dependent on it, subordinate to it, or irrelevant, is an issue that has yet to be conclusively decided.

FAST FACT

Massachusetts representative Elbridge Gerry served as a delegate to the Constitutional Convention but refused to sign the completed Constitution. He was against the "conscientious objector" part of the Second Amendment, because he feared that the national government might declare some people who wanted to serve "scrupulous" and then exclude them from military service.

Congressional Debates over the Second Amendment

FAST FACT

The Senate considered a proposal to add "for the common defense" after "to keep and bear arms," but the motion was not successful. The meaning of this refusal is hotly disputed and can be interpreted in numerous ways.

There was little debate in the first U.S. Congress over the Second Amendment. Most disputes centered on military matters, especially the relationship between militias, standing armies, and liberty. Congress rehashed the familiar questions of the previous twenty years. Were militias superior to standing armies? How could the government best keep the army under civilian control? The role of conscientious objectors was also discussed. In the debates over the Second Amendment, Congress apparently assumed that citizens had a constitutionally protected right (and duty) to serve in militias when called into service. The primary concern seemed to be the need to make sure that state militias would continue to act as a check to the national army, national power, and the threat to freedom that they posed.

The Second Amendment was added to the Constitution in 1791 as part of the Bill of Rights. It attempted to place limits on the power of the newly created federal government by protecting the rights of individual citizens and the states. The right to keep and bear arms was directly related to a person's ability to respond to a call from the government with his own weapons.

"To Keep and Bear Arms"

The second half of the Second Amendment gives the people the right "to keep and bear arms." This peculiar phrase, a translation of the Latin *arma ferre,* is traditionally a military term. "To bear arms" is historically a synonym for serving as a soldier. "Arms" in English usage is not restricted to guns, but applies to weapons in general. The word keeps its military sense in many English phrases: "feat of arms," "brothers in arms," "call to arms," "take up arms," "lay down arms," "an arm of the cavalry," and the "armed forces." "Arms" is a profession that a person chooses and means "the act of soldiering." The discussion of conscientious objectors in Madison's draft and the House version both tie "bearing arms" with giving military service. In this view, the phrase "to keep and bear arms" seems to refer to the militia's permanent readiness.

However, by the late 1810s, the phrase "bear arms" seemed to include self-defense, as well as soldiering; the Bills of Rights of Mississippi, passed in 1817, and Alabama, passed in 1819, both said, "Every citizen has a right to bear arms in defense of himself and the state." Even if Second Amendment rights applied to the militia, the arms themselves were still to be provided, and therefore owned, by individuals. The interpretation of the wording is crucial, especially in modern debates over the Second Amendment, since it is specifically "the right of the people to keep and bear arms" that shall not be infringed, according to the Constitution.

FAST FACT

The Romans did not have guns, but their "arms" included weapons from spears and arrows to swords and siege engines, but especially shields. A *coat of arms* is a shield covered (coated) with a person's or family's unique sign.

The Limited Impact of the Second Amendment

Freedoms in the Bill of Rights have rarely been considered absolute. Free speech does not give the speaker the right to falsely shout "Fire!" in a crowded theater or incite a riot. In terms of the Second Amendment, even extreme defenders of the Bill of Rights do not consider it acceptable for people to have tactical nuclear weapons in their backyards or antiaircraft guns on their roofs. The law recognizes that there is a point when freedom interferes with social order.

Throughout American history, the national, state, and local governments have regulated gun possession (and all weapon usage) in many different ways. Some state and local governments require certain types of guns, or even shooters, to be licensed. The national government outlaws the possession and sale of certain types of firearms, such as machine guns. Any rights granted by the Second Amendment have always been weighed against the needs of the American people at any given historical moment.

The Adaptability of the Constitution

The nation has changed considerably in the more than two centuries since the Constitution was written. Militias have ceased to exist, except in the very different form of the National Guard. Since the end of World War II (1939–1945), an enormous peacetime standing army has become a regular, accepted feature of American life. The possibility suggested by the framers of the Constitution that a professional army might threaten personal liberty in the United States seems unlikely any time in the foreseeable future. Muskets that used to fire three rounds a minute have been replaced by M-16s that fire 500 rounds a minute. Crime is now seen as a major American problem.

In creating the Second Amendment, the framers hardly discussed the personal, private, or individual use of weapons for hunting, recreation, or even self-defense; almost all references deal with the militia and its public functions. Private ownership and use of weapons were simply not an issue for debate in the late 1780s, and it is not surprising that eighteenth-century Americans could not anticipate how arguments over the Second Amendment would play out 200 years later.

The original intentions of the writers of the Second Amendment are very important, but not necessarily decisive. The authors of the Constitution brilliantly recognized that it would not be a document written in stone. They assumed that future generations of Americans would have to adapt the Constitution to meet new conditions. For example, would the framers object to background checks on people who wanted to buy guns to determine if they had criminal histories? Would they view background checks as an infringement on people's fundamental rights? Historical scholarship can propose answers, but it will never end the debate. In the end, the Constitution and the Bill of Rights are living documents. While past interpretations remain important, every generation has an obligation to study the document anew and give it contemporary meaning.

CHAPTER 3

Guns and the Militia in American Culture

The American militia of the type used in the American Revolution gradually faded away in the 1800s. It was replaced by National Guard units that bore little resemblance to the ideals of the framers of the Constitution. Yet individual gun ownership in the United States remained common among men even though it lost all connection to national defense. It's difficult to determine how many people owned guns or the number produced between 1781 and 1960, but it seems safe to say that millions of guns were manufactured, imported, sold, or just given away as surplus after each war.

Although certain restrictions on gun behavior, such as carrying concealed weapons and firing guns in public, were widespread, governments rarely restricted the right to use guns in this period. This reflected the general nineteenth-century belief that the government, especially the national government, should not be involved in Americans' personal lives. This worldview began to change in the early 1900s, but it was the economic crisis of the 1930s that led to the passage of the first national gun control laws. Even then, debates over the meaning of the Second Amendment were limited. Not until the 1960s did passionate argument over the Second Amendment become a regular feature of American life.

The Uniform Militia Act of 1792

After the ratification of the Bill of Rights in 1791, Congress, following the instructions laid down by the Constitution, established rules and procedures to organize the militias. The Uniform Militia Act of 1792 defined the nation's militia as "every free able-bodied white male citizen of the respective states" between the ages of eighteen and forty-five.

Even in colonial times, militias were divided into two groups: the unorganized or *general militias,* and the organized or *select militias.* The general militia was made up of the entire body of eligible males, the "people" as a whole, who were supposed to participate in the minimum required service. The select militias were volunteer units that organized and trained more frequently and often with their own equipment, uniforms, and unit loyalty. The Uniform Militia Act of 1792 attempted to sustain the idea of a nation defended by the citizen-soldiers of the general militia.

FAST FACT

The Militia Act of 1792 remained the basic federal militia law for 111 years, until 1903.

Article I, Section 8, of the Constitution specifically stated that Congress was responsible for arming the militias. The federal government interpreted this to mean only that everyone would carry the same type of weapons. Rather than using scarce tax dollars to arm the soldiers, the government required a militia member to "provide himself with a good musket or firelock, a sufficient bayonet and belt, two spare flints, and a knapsack, [and] a pouch with a box therein to contain no less than twenty-four cartridges." In the two years following the Uniform Militia Act, all fifteen states passed their own laws to bring their militia systems in line with federal guidelines. The Uniform Militia Act, however, did not penalize the states or men who did not follow it, and many of the specific conditions of this act were ignored.

The Calling Forth Act and the Whiskey Rebellion

The Calling Forth Act of 1792 (modified in 1795) explained the role of the militia. This act gave broad powers to the president of the United States to use the state militias to enforce both state and federal laws in case people were not obeying the law or were in open rebellion. The Calling Forth Act did not give the people or the militia any right to rebel against the government. In fact, the act used the exact wording of Article I, Section 8 of the Constitution: "to provide for calling forth the militia to execute the laws of the Union, suppress insurrections and repel invasions."

Sometimes—for example, during the early stages of Shays's Rebellion—a state militia refused to put down a rebellion because it sided with the rebels. In that case, Section 2 of the Calling Forth Act specifically gave the president and Congress the power to use the militias from other states to crush an insurrection.

The Calling Forth Act made it clear that early Congresses never intended militias to be privately formed or used against the government, but instead were a military arm of the government. In Shays's Rebellion, the militias of eastern Massachusetts were used to crush a farmers' revolt against high taxes and the seizing of farms due to unpaid debt. In the South, militias served as the main military forces to keep African-American slaves from rebelling and gaining their freedom.

The Whiskey Rebellion, an uprising in western Pennsylvania in 1794, demonstrated the conservative nature of the early national militia. When Congress passed Alexander Hamilton's tax on whiskey in 1791, some citizens rioted against the federal government's efforts to collect the tax. They claimed that the whiskey tax hurt them economically and took away their liberty. Rioters compared themselves to the patriots of the American Revolution, who opposed British efforts to limit American freedom. The rioters had fought for freedom once, and they were willing to do it again.

The rebels received no sympathy from the federal government, however. Even leading antifederalists supported putting down this threat to domestic security. George Washington issued a call for 13,000 militiamen from Pennsylvania, Maryland, Virginia, and New Jersey. Resistance vanished in the face of this overwhelming force, led by Washington himself, and the rebellion was crushed. The new government's power to enforce its laws and collect taxes had been established through the power of the federalized militia.

The War of 1812: Militias Fail the Nation

The reputation of the citizen militias suffered a crippling blow as a result of their terrible performance in the War of 1812. Even as a supplement to the regular army, the state militia system was almost useless in that conflict. Poorly

Daniel Morgan (1736–1802) led some of the forces called in to stop the Whiskey Rebellion in western Pennsylvania in 1794. Morgan had also been a commander during the Revolution. The Whiskey Rebellion was the first time the federal government commandeered state militias to keep peace in another state.

trained and ill-equipped militias rarely matched the discipline of well-trained British veterans of the bloody Napoleonic Wars (1799–1815) in Europe. After the War of 1812, Americans would never count on militias again, indirectly beginning the debate on the meaning of the Second Amendment. The amendment, by somehow tying the right to keep and bear arms to service in the militia, opened the possibility that the right to keep and bear arms no longer had any constitutional protection if the militias ceased to exist.

The American militia hardly covered itself in glory in the War of 1812. At the Battle of Queenstown Heights, the New York militia refused to leave the state and join the battle in Canada, even though its presence would have been a great advantage to the American side. Winfield Scott, later to become one of the greatest generals in American history, fought at the battle, and his contempt for the militiamen knew no bounds. "These vermin," he wrote, "who infest all republics, boastful enough at home, no sooner found themselves in sight of the enemy than they discovered that the militia of the United States could not be constitutionally marched into a foreign country." In New England, the opposition to what residents contemptuously called "Mr. Madison's War" was so great that the governors of these states refused to surrender their militias to the national government, even when commanded by President Madison.

The British attack on and burning of Washington, D.C., in 1814 was perhaps the most dramatic and humiliating episode in the War of 1812. It proved once and for all that the poorly trained state militias that the United States relied on were no match for the professional soldiers from Great Britain.

Perhaps the most embarrassing performance of the militia was in defense of the capital of the United States. When the British attacked Washington, D.C., in August 1814 with an expeditionary force of less than 5,000 men, the vaunted militia crumbled. Although 90,000

militiamen were summoned, only 7,000 appeared. After suffering less than 100 casualties, the American militia broke and ran; thousands quietly slipped away for home without ever firing a shot. The British then easily occupied Washington and burned the government buildings with almost no resistance. While fleeing the burning capital, perhaps President Madison recalled his discussion in *The Federalist Papers*—how no nation could ever be defeated that boasted a militia of 500,000 armed male citizens fighting for their common liberties and bravely supporting the government that represented them.

After the failure of the militia in the War of 1812, Gouverneur Morris, who had been a delegate at the Constitutional Convention in 1787, wrote that the framers had actually never believed in the strength of the militia, which he compared to leaning "on a broken reed." With the benefit of hindsight, Morris claimed,

> An overweening vanity leads the fond many...to believe or affect to believe, that militia can beat veteran troops in the open field and even play of battle.... But to rely on undisciplined, ill-officered men, though each were individually as brave as Caesar, to resist the well-directed impulse of veterans, is to act in defiance of reason and experience.

FAST FACT

When Congress declared war on Britain in June of 1812, President Madison placed his faith in the citizen-soldiers of the state militias. The official U.S. Army at that time consisted of only 7,000 men, while in Europe at the same time, the English Duke of Wellington commanded 46,000 men at the Battle of Salamanca, and Napoleon led an army of 400,000 into Poland.

The Decline of the Militias

Neither the federal government nor the states continued universal militia training and service after the disasters of the War of 1812. The U.S. Army remained small throughout the 1800s—numbering between 6,000 and 27,000 in peacetime—but most Americans agreed that this army, and not the state militias, represented the core force for national defense. The national government continued taking over more of the role of making war; in the mid-1800s, the United States began to provide firearms, uniforms, and other supplies to the select militias. No militia forces were used at all in the Mexican War (1846–1848), which was fought in a foreign country.

In the American Civil War, when both sides needed every man they could find, both the Union and the Confederacy resorted to the use of the militia once more. Because no one believed anymore that military service should be a duty of all able-bodied white males, Civil War militias were actually volunteer military companies—essentially select militias. When the war proved bloodier and longer than either side expected, both the Union and the Confederacy turned to military drafts to fill out their large armies. The draft proved to be very controversial, but it would be used numerous times in the twentieth century to provide soldiers when there were not enough citizens willing to join the American army.

Although the militias were not employed in battle, social aspects of the militia system continued through the nineteenth century in many states. Local militias, like volunteer fire companies, continued to get together for "musters" long after their official duties disappeared. These gatherings served mostly social purposes and often took place at local taverns. Instead of depending on these militiamen, the U.S. government relied on its professional army and an elite corps of volunteers that made up a select militia.

Increased industrialization in the United States after the Civil War led to class warfare and labor violence, such as the great railroad strikes of 1877. As a result, state governments took new interest in their local military forces. These governments did not even pretend to revive the idea of a militia of all able-bodied men. Instead, they worked hard to organize volunteer military units and convince "respectable" citizens to join or support these select militias to put down the workers. These organized volunteer companies began to call themselves "national guards" to make it clear that they were not related to the disreputable, unorganized militias that were meeting in the local taverns. In the late 1800s, individual states placed these state National Guard units in huge, fortress-like armories in large and even medium-sized cities. The armories were then used as command centers to break strikes and control labor unrest.

The National Guard Becomes the Militia

When Theodore Roosevelt became president in 1901, only three years had passed since he had won a heroic military reputation in the Spanish-American War (1898). Having seen battle firsthand, Roosevelt declared in 1901 that "our militia law is obsolete and worthless."

Congress finally changed the old system, beginning with the Militia Act of 1903, also known as the Dick Act. This Militia Act legally separated the organized militia, now recognized by federal law as the National Guard, from the reserve militia. The act provided for federal arming, training, and drilling of the National Guard but said nothing at all about the unorganized militia, which had essentially ceased to exist. In 1916, Congress passed the National Defense Act, which commanded the state National Guards to follow federal rules and procedures and organize themselves in the same way as the regular army.

In the twentieth century, the United States expanded its concept of national defense. The American military no longer waited at the border to repel foreign invaders. The place of the United States in world affairs changed beyond the wildest imaginations of the framers of the Constitution and the Bill of Rights. American soldiers were sent all over the world: Europe, Asia, the Caribbean, Central and South America, Africa, and the Middle East. Beginning with the Cold War in 1945—a war of ideas with the Soviet Union (present-day Russia) for influence around the world, which lasted until the early 1990s—an enormous standing army of more than 1 million soldiers has become a regular, accepted feature of American life. Military intervention by this large army now typically takes place by presidential order; Congress has not issued a declaration of war since 1941.

Since World War I (1914–1918), the National Guards have been trained by each individual state but operated under federal regulation. The National Guard and the U.S. Army together now make up the forces assigned to meet America's military needs. In modern wars, such as in World War I, World War II, the Korean War (1950–1953), and the Vietnam War (1964–1975), shortages of willing soldiers were met by the selective service system (the military draft) and not by re-creating eighteenth-century-style militias.

In the twenty-first century, the National Guard's equipment is the same as the U.S. Army's, and the federal government pays members for the time that they spend in training. In peacetime, the state government controls the National Guard and uses it to put down local riots or to help in times of natural disasters. In times of war, the National Guard is absorbed into the active service of the United States and the president is its commander in chief. Units of the National Guard were called out for the Korean War, the Berlin crisis of 1961, the first Persian Gulf War (1991), and the war in Iraq (2003). However, Congress still has the option of mobilizing a militia force of all able-bodied men from age seventeen (changed from eighteen in 1956) to forty-five based upon the idea of universal service in the reserve militia.

The Hunting Tradition

Despite changes in the role of the militia, many Americans owned firearms in the nineteenth century. The hunting tradition remained important, especially in the South and in the West, although the popularity of hunting in American history is disputed. Hunting animals provided a source of food for rural Americans, but it was much more efficient to kill domestic livestock for meat than to go chasing after deer. Trapping was an important economic activity, far more efficient than hunting. Men often hunted as a leisure activity.

Commercial hunting was also widespread in the 1800s, resulting in such tragedies as the extinction of the once-common passenger pigeon (3 billion to 5 billion killed) and the near-extinction of the buffalo (an estimated 50

FAST FACT

The American passenger pigeon was once the most abundant bird species on earth; Americans with guns wiped it out in a century. The last one, a bird named Martha, died in the Cincinnati Zoo on September 1, 1914.

million killed). Guns made hunting possible on a scale undreamed of by Native Americans. On one day in 1875, Tom Nixon, a professional hunter, killed 120 buffalo in forty minutes with a rifle; from September 15 to October 20, Nixon killed 2,127 buffalo.

By the time of the 1920 census, the majority of Americans lived in cities. The hunting tradition began to decline in the face of the urbanization and suburbanization of the United States, the loss of open space, and the decreasing percentage of rural populations. A 2001 survey indicated that there were 13 million hunters in the United States (representing about 6 percent of the population), and the number appeared to be shrinking.

Firearms on the Frontier

The United States has a frontier heritage. (The *frontier* is the part of a country that forms the furthest limits of its settled or inhabited regions.) As the United States expanded westward, settlers moved into sparsely populated regions. Here, whites confronted people whom they wanted to remove, or whose land they wanted, such as Native Americans and Mexicans.

FAST FACT

The frontier experience is not unique to the United States. Countries as different as Russia, Argentina, Canada, and Australia also had frontiers but evolved cultures quite different from those of the United States and each other.

Contrary to myth, six-shooters and rifles played little part in this drama. The West was "won" by the sheer number of ranchers and farmers, transported and supplied by transcontinental railroads, who flooded the area between the Mississippi River and the Pacific Ocean in the half-century between 1840 and 1890. The white population between the Mississippi and the Pacific increased from 7 million in 1870 to 17 million in 1890. The number of farms in the United States jumped from 2 million on the eve of the Civil War to almost 6 million in 1900.

The West was also an urban frontier; by 1890, the percentage of people living in cities of 10,000 or more in the West was greater than in any other section of the country except the Northeast. In the Western cattle towns, crime and vigilantes (people who take the law into their own hands) were only briefly tolerated. Many Western

FAST FACT

Local militias often committed some of the most shameful atrocities in the West. On November 29, 1864, a Colorado militia under the command of Colonel John Chivington attacked a group of peaceful Cheyenne at Sand Creek, where they had gathered under the governor's protection. "We must kill them big and little," Chivington said. The militia slaughtered about 150 Cheyenne, mostly women and children, many of whom were taking refuge under an American flag.

towns prohibited cowboys from carrying their guns into town, and there were few homicides. For example, in the most violent cattle towns—Abilene, Caldwell, Dodge City, Ellsworth, and Wichita—only forty-five killings were recorded between 1870 and 1885; in six of those years, no killings were recorded at all. Gunfights were particularly rare. Although thirty-nine of the victims died from gunshot wounds, less than a third of them returned fire, and many of them were apparently unarmed.

When settlers came into conflict with Native Americans, they generally did not rely on their own organizations or militias, but pleaded or demanded that the federal government send the U.S. Army to defend them. Most of the killing that took place on the frontier involved small-scale warfare between Native Americans and the army. This fighting cost millions of dollars (military spending was 60 percent of the 1880 budget) and the lives of twenty-five U.S. soldiers for every Native American. It was the U.S. Army, and not the rugged individual settler with a gun, that was responsible for the military defeat of Native Americans on the Plains.

The Racial Question

The question of the Second Amendment and gun use in the United States also has a racial dimension. In the South in the years before the Civil War, the militia's main purpose was to preserve white supremacy and keep blacks enslaved. Slave patrols, which did routine policing, were drawn from militia rosters. Obviously, Southern states forbade slaves from carrying firearms, but also outlawed the ownership of guns by free blacks. In 1844, the North Carolina Supreme Court ruled unanimously that laws restricting the use of firearms by free blacks did not violate the Second Amendment.

This racial aspect made a brief appearance in Justice Roger Taney's decision in the infamous Dred Scott case of 1857. Among other issues, the U.S. Supreme Court ruled that free African-Americans were not citizens of the

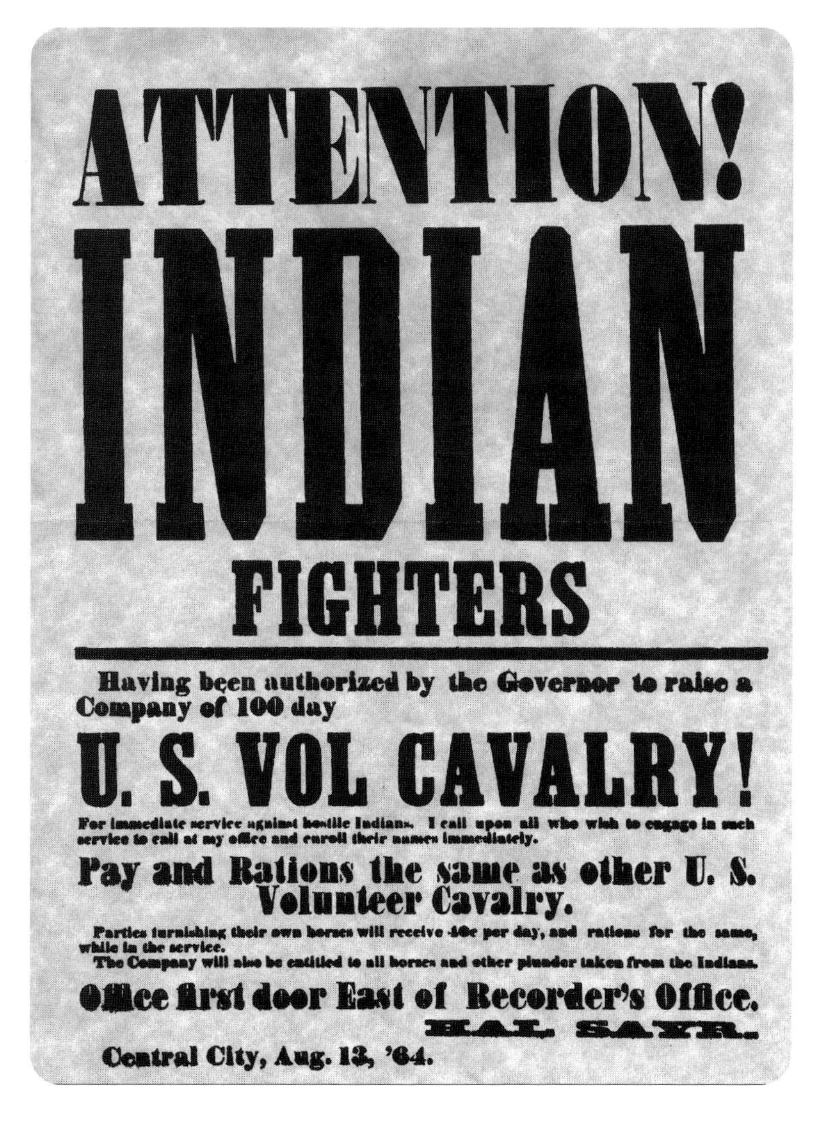

This poster, dated August 13, 1864, advertises for volunteers to join a cavalry (a group of horse-mounted soldiers). The cavalry, commanded by Colonel John Chivington, would participate in the so-called Sand Creek Massacre, at which many dozens of Native Americans were killed.

United States and had no rights under the Constitution "which a white man was bound to respect." The decision, usually considered the most blatantly racist and most poorly researched and reasoned decision in the history of the Supreme Court, specifically noted that if free blacks were citizens of the United States, they would have "the full liberty of freedom of speech in public and in private...and to keep and carry arms wherever they went." The judicial value of this pronouncement is greatly disputed, but the underlying sentiment is clear; Southern whites like Taney found it unacceptable for free black people to be walking around with guns.

After the Civil War, a virtual race war broke out in many parts of the South. This period, known as Reconstruction, ended with the newly freed African-Americans being held to second-class status as citizens. For the next century, blacks were prevented from voting in the South, and laws known as Jim Crow laws forced them to use separate and unequal resources and services. The fact that white people (who made up two-thirds of the population of the eleven old Confederate states) owned or controlled the possession of weapons helped them intimidate African-Americans, creating a racial terror-state in the South.

During Reconstruction, Congress thought that blacks would be better able to fend off white attacks if they could acquire and keep weapons. In Section 14 of the Freedmen's Bureau Act of 1866, Congress declared that "the constitutional right to bear arms shall be secured to and enjoyed by all classes." Of course, like many Reconstruction efforts that sought to help the newly freed slaves, this provision was never effectively implemented. If African-Americans had had equal access to weapons, it is possible that they might have been in a better position to resist their reduction to slavery and second-class citizenship. It is also possible that the possession of weapons by a minority group with no rights would be a formula for a race war in which the oppressors would win, as in the case of Native Americans (who possessed firearms, but to no avail). Without a doubt, however, white Southerners used gun ownership to oppress blacks and gun control laws to deny blacks the right of self-protection among most other civil rights.

Increased Social Disorder in Cities

As the United States became increasingly urbanized between 1820 and 1900, there was an increase in crime and social disorder. Cities threw together people of all social types and contrasted at close quarters the vast wealth of some and the intense poverty of others. Urban settings seemed to break down the social restraints of village life and were filled with class, ethnic, and religious tension. Racism, nativism (opposition to immigrants), anti-abolitionism (opposition to people who wanted to free the slaves), and bad feelings between immigrant groups all led to rioting. Criminals and gangs also frightened city-dwellers. Although the use of guns was initially rare, Americans began to regularly use firearms against each other by the 1840s. Street fights or riots among volunteer firemen became occasions for men to pull out pistols or even muskets.

Before the 1840s, cities used constables, watchmen, sheriff's posses, and the militia to keep public order through a system that dated back to the Middle Ages. Posses and the militia, however, required hours, if not days, to assemble. They lacked discipline, disliked taking orders, and sometimes openly sympathized with rioters. Watchmen and constables, appointed by politicians as a way of returning favors, were often incompetent. Many "moonlighted"—that is, they took a night position as a second job and, as a result, often fell asleep at their posts. Sheriffs, aldermen, and marshals made most of their money from fees for serving papers; they did not patrol streets seeking out crime or disturbances. Nonetheless, there was some support to keep things just as they were. Many Americans worried that a police force would make lifestyle arrests, such as jailing people for opening their stores on Sunday or for drinking beer.

FAST FACT

Many watchmen were old men of the lower classes who could not do strenuous work, and they were sometimes the butt of jokes, insults, and pranks (such as the tipping over of the watch house).

The Creation of the Police

Some Americans looked to Great Britain for a new system for preventing outbreaks of violence. In London, food riots, protests against the increasing use of machines in industry, and rising crime had resulted in the Metropolitan Police Act of 1829, which created a city police force. These new "bobbies" (named after their chief sponsor, Prime Minister Robert Peel) were full-time professionals; they could not hold other jobs, participate in politics, or even vote until the 1880s. At first, police officers faced tremendous public hostility; Londoners feared that they would undermine

New York City established its first true police force in 1845. Police forces were forming all over the country during the mid-nineteenth century in response to violence in the cities and the need to keep order. These New York City mounted police officers were photographed during a parade in 1897.

freedom, and workers regarded them as enemies. Eventually, their hard work gained the public's support, especially because they patrolled without guns.

American cities also began to organize police forces in response to group violence and a rise in crime. Boston supplemented part-time watchmen with police in 1837, and New York City replaced its watchmen completely in 1845. Other major cities followed: New Orleans, Louisiana, and Cincinnati, Ohio, in 1852, Philadelphia in 1854, Chicago, Illinois, in 1855, and Baltimore, Maryland, in 1857. By the 1870s, all major cities had professional police forces, and by 1900, so did almost every smaller city. Competing groups, such as watchmen and constables, were disbanded.

Unlike their British cousins, American police generally carried guns. When the newly organized preventive police had begun patrolling American streets, they were armed only with nightsticks. By the 1850s, however, individual police officers began to carry guns, regardless of public opinion and official orders. The weapons helped them better confront armed lawbreakers. In some cases, as in Philadelphia, the city councils authorized their police to carry pistols. Usually, however, this type of permission only confirmed what the police were already doing.

The American public accepted armed police because there seemed little choice, given the widespread presence of guns in the United States and people's willingness to use them. Many urban dwellers, however, continued to regard the police with suspicion. American police were notorious for their readiness to use force, but the crime rate in America also seems to have been far greater than in Western European nations.

The creation of organized urban police forces changed the way that the Second Amendment was viewed by altering the interpretation of the common-law right to carry weapons. This right had been established when there was no effective police and individual citizens were forced to protect themselves. Now that there was an armed police force, to what degree did citizens still possess a right to own their own guns?

Guns and Popular Fiction

Stories involving heroes and violence are common in most cultures of the world. In American popular culture, these heroes often carried guns. Davy Crockett, a real frontiersman, was the subject of many exaggerated books and pamphlets in the period before the Civil War. These wildly popular works combined tall-tale humor with vivid images of guns and violence against women, Native Americans, and escaped slaves.

Inexpensive books known as "dime novels" dominated American popular fiction from 1840 to 1900. These books, like the earlier ones about Davy Crockett, were bought mainly by city dwellers. Most of the stories told very patriotic tales of fighting natives and frontier life. Although real-life Western outlaws were rare, newspaper and fiction writers invented them by the dozen to fascinate eastern readers. This type of fiction romanticized and exaggerated

FAST FACT

The very first feature-length film, *The Great Train Robbery* in 1903, astonished viewers with its realism. When an outlaw in the film aimed his gun at the camera and fired, inexperienced moviegoers supposedly ducked, thinking that the shot was real.

the importance of guns in the settling of the West. For example, the dime novels elevated the Western marshal—in reality an unglamorous character who rounded up drunks and stray dogs—into a heroic gunslinger who defended justice with a six-shooter. Popular novels with Western themes, such as *The Virginian,* Owen Wister's best-selling 1902 novel about Wyoming cowhands, and Zane Grey's popular *Riders of the Purple Sage* of 1912, raised the gun-toting Westerner to the status of an American hero.

Early motion pictures also used violence with firearms to engage viewers. Movies popularized the view that guns were an essential part of America's history and American culture. The most famous blockbuster movie of the early motion picture period, *The Birth of a Nation* (1916), thrilled viewers

Guns have always been part of popular culture, from the dime novels of the nineteenth century to the earliest motion pictures. The 1916 film The Birth of a Nation, *which depicted guns as an integral part of United States history, sent messages about gun use that by today's standards are very negative.*

with its imitation Civil War battle scenes. This movie offered the view that violent intimidation with guns was an excellent way to keep black Americans from voting in the South.

Firearms, Gangsters, and the 1920s

Even with the creation of the police, many Americans expressed dismay at the rising toll of handgun-related murders. Especially in urban areas, the number of these homicides had been rising since the 1890s. In New York, the state legislature passed the Sullivan Law in 1911 in response to the murder of New York City mayor William Gaynor by a discharged employee the previous year. The Sullivan Law placed strict requirements on the sale, possession, and carrying of concealed weapons. New York residents now needed a police permit both to own and to carry a pistol.

The Sullivan Law did not stop urban violence, especially after the Eighteenth Amendment (the prohibition of alcohol) took effect in 1920. Many people simply refused to obey Prohibition, even if it was in the Constitution. Residents of large cities, whose ethnic populations had always opposed Prohibition, went to speakeasies (illegal private clubs), indirectly supporting liquor smugglers, or made their own gin in the bathtub. Organized crime, which controlled the illegal production and sale of liquor to a great degree, became a huge business in the United States.

Although there is some dispute as to whether the crime rate actually rose in the 1920s, a series of spectacular murders in Chicago convinced Americans that it did. Competition between criminal gangs was fierce with so much money at stake in the illegal alcohol business. Dion O'Bannon, the leader of Chicago's North Side Gang, was gunned down in 1924 in a flower shop; two months later, his gang avenged the death by pumping five bullets into Johnny Torrio (who survived, but then retired). In 1925, eleven cars filled with Hymie Weiss's men drove by Al Capone's headquarters and fired 1,000 bullets into the building; in return, Weiss was killed by machine gun fire in

FAST FACT

Al Capone's Chicago crime organization collected more than $100 million in 1927 alone. Although Capone was blamed for many brutal murders, he eventually served jail time only for federal income tax evasion.

1926. The sequence climaxed with the infamous Saint Valentine's Day Massacre of 1929, in which Capone's gang killed seven members of the North Side Gang. More than 250 violent deaths bloodied Chicago between 1920 and 1927; Capone was said to employ as many as 1,000 gunmen.

This rise of gangsters in the 1920s led to a national debate over gun control. Reformers proposed the licensing of gun owners and the outright banning of pistols. Opponents of this proposal argued that a handgun ban would interfere with personal liberty and infringe on the inalienable right of self-defense. The Second Amendment, however, was rarely mentioned; the right of self-defense was apparently not considered to be dependent on the Second Amendment.

Horace Kephart, in an article in *Outing* magazine in 1922, vehemently argued against the pistol ban. Using anti–gun control arguments that would hardly change over the next eighty years, Kephart claimed that it was "silly to blame the instrument for the deed.... If we must pass a nationwide law about pistols, let it be a law that encourages reputable citizens to get the best ones and train themselves to use them right, and that makes it as difficult as possible for disreputable citizens to get arms equally good."

Gun groups often supported tighter restrictions. The United States Revolver Association, an organization of amateur experts in the use of revolvers, was a leading force in writing gun laws. In 1923, California, North Dakota, and New Hampshire all adopted firearms legislation based on the U.S. Revolver Association's recommendations. Strict gun control laws were widely debated in the press, in state capitals, and in Congress in the 1920s. However, the federal government acted only to ban the mail-order sale of handguns to individuals in 1927. Americans of the 1920s generally believed that the national government should stay out of policy matters; if any changes were necessary, they could be done at the state level. This attitude toward gun control would change during the 1930s.

The illegal, often violent activities of Chicago gangster Al Capone and others like him in the 1920s prompted much debate over gun control and the right of people to own handguns. At this time, however, the Second Amendment was not invoked by those opposed to gun control.

The Gangster Movie and Censorship

When the American economy collapsed during the Great Depression, which began in 1929, gangsters achieved a sort of grudging respect, especially in the movies. *The Public Enemy,* starring James Cagney, and *Little Caesar,* featuring Edward G. Robinson, both appeared in 1930, followed by *Smart Money* in 1931 and *Scarface* in 1932. People flocked to theaters to see gangsters gun down their opponents.

Many gangster films were box office smashes. They typically focused on individual criminals, generally of lower-class immigrant background, who were driven by a desire for power and wealth and whose ambitions led to their downfall. In a sense, these films were updated rags-to-riches stories in which the American dream of upward mobility now took place outside the law and involved aggression and guns.

Many critics condemned this seeming glorification of gangsters, and there were hearings in Congress regarding violence in popular culture. Censors and civic leaders feared that criminal actions on the screen might inspire similar actions off the screen, especially among young people. As a result, Hollywood studios established the Production Code Administration (PCA) in 1934 to make rules for all films. The PCA's new code, which was strictly enforced, stated that "law, natural or human, shall not be ridiculed," that "correct standards of life...shall be presented," and that the "sympathy of the audience shall never be thrown to the side of crime, wrong-doing, evil, or sin."

From 1934 to 1968, the American movie industry glorified the Federal Bureau of Investigation (FBI), lawmen, and cowboys. Guns and violence were acceptable to censors as long as the good guys won. The actors who had formerly portrayed gangsters kept their guns but now joined the heroic federal government. Cagney in *G-Men* in 1935 and Robinson in *Bullets or Ballots* in 1936 were still tough, but worked for and not against law and order. Hollywood's revival of the cowboy film also reinforced the idea that guns were acceptable, provided that they were in the right hands. The Production Code was not abolished until 1968, when the popularity of television and foreign films forced Hollywood to become more daring in order to attract viewers.

Change in Federal Policy Toward Guns

During the Great Depression, the federal government became more involved in the health and welfare of the American people than at any previous time. While governor of New York, Franklin Roosevelt had strongly supported handgun licensing laws and the banning of machine guns. When he was elected president in 1932, Roosevelt appointed gun control supporter Homer Cummings as his attorney general. Cummings believed that all firearms should be registered; he said, "Show me the man who does not want his gun registered, and I will show you a man who should not have a gun."

Many Americans had come to believe that violence had increased dramatically in the 1920s and 1930s. The dangers of automatic weapons seemed beyond dispute during the early days of the Depression. The adventures of exciting criminals such as Charles "Pretty Boy" Floyd, George "Machine Gun" Kelly, and Bonnie Parker and Clyde Barrow fascinated, entertained, and horrified the nation. Then on February 15, 1933, Giuseppe Zangara attempted to assassinate President-elect Roosevelt while he was giving a speech in Miami, Florida. Zangara, who had bought his handgun for four dollars at a local drugstore, failed to harm Roosevelt, but he killed Anton Cermak, the mayor of Chicago.

As a result of both gangsterism and political assassination, a bill was placed before Congress in 1933 that would regulate the sale of so-called gangster-type weapons and require the registration of all handguns.

The National Firearms Act of 1934

The National Firearms Act of 1934 taxed the manufacture, sale, and transfer of certain weapons and accessories: sawed-off shotguns, sawed-off rifles, machine guns, and silencers. In addition, the act set very strict rules relating to the purchasing and licensing of such weapons. Purchasers of weapons had to undergo background checks by the FBI, submit their photographs, and provide full fingerprinting. Each weapon purchased under the law had to be registered. The legislation also required the seller of the weapon to pay a transfer tax of $200, a fee that was usually passed on to the buyer. Finally, if the federal authorities approved the purchase, the buyer also needed to receive clearance from a local law enforcement officer to bring the weapon into a local area.

The Roosevelt administration had originally intended to include a plan for the registration of all handguns for a one-dollar fee but dropped the idea when the firearms industry and the National Rifle Association (NRA) objected to it. The NRA supported the fight against gangsterism but had urged its members to write Congress opposing handgun registration. The flood of letters was crucial in the decision to delete the phrase "all weaponry" and replace it with "machine guns and sawed-off shotguns."

Since the passage of the National Firearms Act in 1934, more than 175,000 of the restricted weapons have been registered. It was this law that led to the Supreme Court case of *United States v. Miller* in 1939, the last time that the U.S. Supreme Court ruled solely on Second Amendment issues.

In a final flurry of gun control legislation, Congress passed the Federal Firearms Act of 1938. This act attempted to regulate the interstate sale of guns. It required manufacturers, dealers, and importers of firearms (and ammunition for pistols and revolvers) to receive a federal license. A fee for the license would be paid to the Internal Revenue Service. The law also prohibited sales and delivery of firearms to known criminals.

The Calm Before the Storm

The public's interest in firearms regulation in the 1930s followed the highly publicized gun violence of the 1920s and 1930s. The 1940s and 1950s lacked this kind of gangsterism and political assassination. Moreover, when 9 million veterans came home after World War II, many had a new interest in firearms. Hunting and target shooting surged in popularity, and the issue of the role of guns in American life attracted little attention.

Thirty years after the Federal Firearms Act of 1938, widespread rioting and several notorious political assassinations once more led to calls for stricter firearms legislation. The passage of the Gun Control Act of 1968 represented a change in the history of the Second Amendment in American culture. From that time on, the debate over gun control and the right to keep and bear arms has become a virtually permanent feature of life in the United States.

CHAPTER 4

Gun Control Legislation and the Right to Keep and Bear Arms

FAST FACT

The Federal Aviation Act of 1958, which banned anyone from carrying a gun onto a passenger plane, represented a rare federal attempt to control gun use in the quarter-century before 1968.

Americans have close to 200 million guns and several hundred gun control laws. Until the 1960s, arguments over the Second Amendment and gun control did not play a major part in American politics or culture. There were very few national laws that dealt with guns; the National Firearms Act of 1934 marked the high point of federal control of gun use in the United States until 1968. No part of the extremely weak Federal Firearms Act of 1938 produced more than a hundred arrests per year.

After the Korean War, the situation began to change. Surplus army weapons from the war flooded the United States. In the 1960s, the crime rate began to rise, slowly at first, and then faster and faster. "If it bleeds, it leads" (meaning if there was violence involved, it would make a good story) became the motto of television news coverage. Every day, increasing numbers of television viewers could watch reports featuring murders somewhere in the United States by casual strangers, embittered family members, and snipers. Television constantly reported on crime and gun violence, because they were dramatic, easy to cover, and required almost no background knowledge by either reporter or viewer. Americans no longer feared a standing army, but their neighbors down the street now made them extremely nervous. Increased political violence in the 1960s, in the form of assassinations and race riots, brought these trends to a climax in the Gun Control Act of 1968.

Political Assassinations in the 1960s

The 1960s were a turbulent decade filled with political violence. In 1963, President John F. Kennedy was shot and killed while riding in a motorcade in Dallas, Texas—the first president to be assassinated in sixty-two years. His alleged killer, Lee Harvey Oswald, supposedly purchased his rifle through a mail-order advertisement in an NRA publication. A few days later, while being transferred in police custody, Oswald was shot and killed by Jack Ruby on live national television while a horrified nation looked

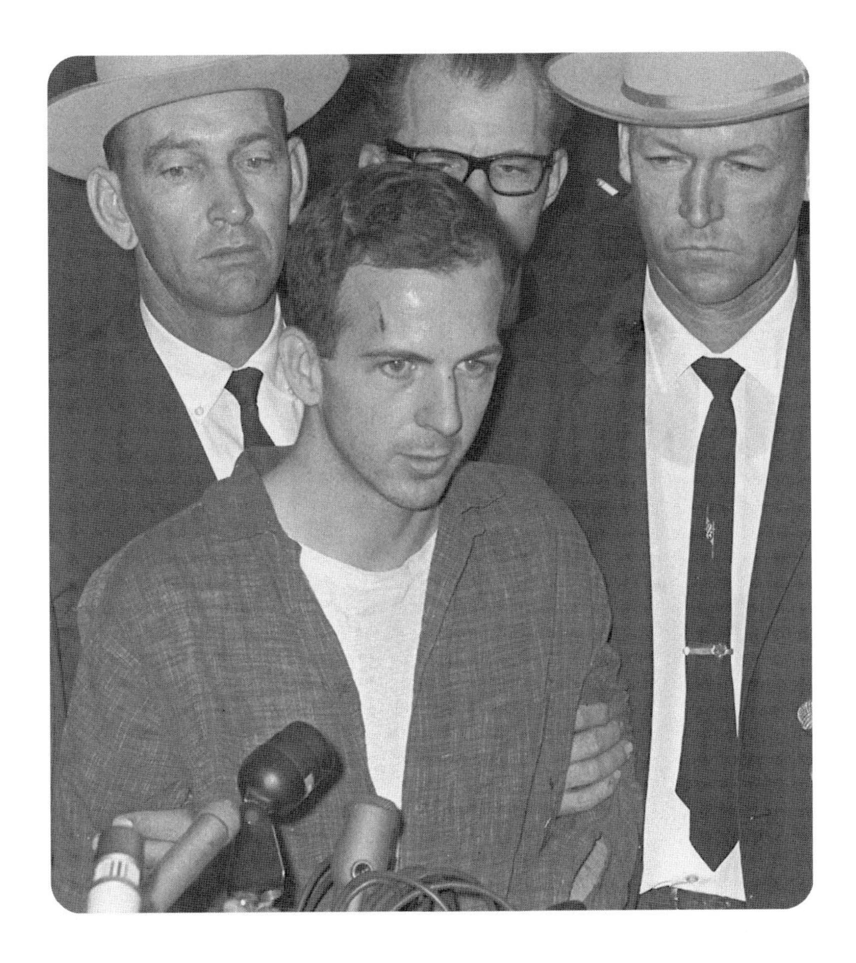

Lee Harvey Oswald, accused killer of President John F. Kennedy, speaks to reporters in Dallas, Texas, the day after Kennedy was killed in 1963. Oswald had just been formally charged with the murder. The next day, Oswald himself was shot by Jack Ruby, a killing seen by millions of Americans on live television.

on. John F. Kennedy's brother, Robert, was a U.S. senator from New York. When he ran for president in 1968, he was murdered while leaving a hotel after winning the California presidential primary.

Nor were these the only high-profile assassinations. In 1965, Malcolm X, the influential African-American leader who supported armed self-defense for blacks, was shot and killed before speaking in a public auditorium in New York City. In 1968, Martin Luther King Jr., the civil rights leader who preached pacifism and nonviolence, was murdered by a sniper as he stood on the balcony of a hotel in Memphis, Tennessee.

These were certainly not the first assassinations in American history. Presidents Abraham Lincoln in 1865, James Garfield in 1881, and William McKinley in 1901 had all been shot and killed with handguns, while assassins had tried but failed to murder both Theodore

FAST FACT

Massachusetts senator Edward Kennedy, the last surviving Kennedy brother, became a strong supporter of gun control. He said, "Our complex society requires a rethinking of the proper role of firearms in modern America. Our forefathers used firearms as an integral part of their struggle for survival. But today, firearms are not appropriate for daily life in the United States."

and Franklin Roosevelt. In the 1960s, however, the concentration of so many political killings in five short years turned American attention to the issue of gun control and the Second Amendment.

Long Hot Summers

Racial violence also tore America apart in the 1960s. Riots often began with a police incident. In African-American neighborhoods, the police represented white government power; in 1967, more than 30 percent of the population of Detroit, Michigan, and Cleveland, Ohio, was black, but only 5 percent and 7 percent of police officers, respectively, were black. Police brutality and prejudice toward African-Americans were common, and many black citizens viewed the police almost as an army of occupation. Because race riots often occurred in hot weather, when people were uncomfortable and tension was high, the riot-filled period from 1964 to 1968 was known as the years of the "long hot summers."

A National Guardsman stands at an intersection in a Detroit neighborhood during a riot in July 1967. Many of the riots that swept through American cities throughout the 1960s were touched off by police actions. The horror of the riots led many people to call for tougher gun laws.

A small riot in Harlem, a neighborhood of New York City, in 1964 was the first in the sequence of riots. The first large-scale riot occurred in the area known as Watts in Los Angeles in 1965. An estimated 30,000 rioters participated, scattered over a 46-square-mile (120-square-kilometer) area; it took 1,600 police and 14,000 National Guard troops to restore order. The final tally read: 34 killed, 1,032 injured, 3,952 arrested; property damage estimated at $40 million; and 1,000 buildings burned, looted, damaged, or destroyed.

The next year, there were twenty-one disturbances, including a major riot in Hough in Cleveland. In 1967, more than seventy major racial incidents marred the summer, even in small cities such as Waterloo, Iowa, and Dayton, Ohio. In Newark, New Jersey, the National Guard and local police fired 13,000 rounds of ammunition in an attempt to restore order during a series of riots. In Detroit, an enormous riot left 43 dead and 700 injured. More than 1,600 fires were set, resulting in $50 million in property damage. The riots, assassinations, and rising crime rates all lent support to the idea of restricting the number of guns in America.

The Gun Control Act of 1968

The Gun Control Act and the Omnibus Crime Control and Safe Streets Act of 1968, enacted during the administration of President Lyndon Johnson, were controversial laws that passed Congress only after long, bitter debate. They were much stricter than any previous weapons laws and affected how guns were bought and used in the United States in many ways. The most important restriction was the prohibition of the sale of guns and ammunition by mail to out-of-state residents.

These federal laws also banned gun ownership by many different classes of people: felons, fugitives from justice, illegal drug users, minors, the mentally ill, dishonorably discharged veterans, illegal aliens, and those who had renounced their American citizenship. Manufacturers,

FAST FACT

NRA president Harold Glasser testified before the Senate on the Gun Control Act. He warned that the legislation was part of an effort to "foist upon an unsuspecting and aroused public a law that would, through its operation, sound the death knell for the shooting sport and eventually disarm the American public."

importers, and dealers in firearms now had to pay increased licensing fees. All guns were required to have serial numbers, and the federal government promised to enforce stricter record-keeping practices. Purchasers of handguns had to be at least twenty-one years old, and purchasers of long guns had to be at least eighteen. The importation of "Saturday night specials" (cheap handguns) was prohibited, as were some types of semiautomatic assault weapons and two types of military shotguns. Crimes of violence that involved carrying and using firearms when dealing drugs now carried stricter penalties.

Some critics of this legislation claimed that it was an unconstitutional violation of the Second Amendment. However, the U.S. government's position had already been made clear in the report of the President's Commission on Law Enforcement and Administration of Justice in 1967. The report claimed,

> The U.S. Supreme Court and lower Federal courts have consistently interpreted this Amendment only as a prohibition against Federal interference with the State militia and not as a guarantee of an individual's right to keep or carry firearms.... The argument that the Second Amendment prohibits State or Federal regulation of citizen ownership of firearms has no validity whatsoever.

The congressional authors of the Gun Control Act went out of their way to make sure that the purpose of the legislation was not misunderstood. Section 101 stated that

> it is not the purpose of this title to place any undue or unnecessary Federal restrictions or burdens on law-abiding citizens with respect to the acquisition, possession, or use of firearms appropriate to the purpose of hunting, trap-shooting, target shooting, personal protection, or any other lawful activity, and that this title is not intended to discourage or eliminate the private ownership or use of firearms by law-abiding citizens for lawful purposes.

The Early Years of the NRA

The National Rifle Association (NRA) of America is by far the most influential lobbying organization for gun use in the United States. (To *lobby* is to try to influence lawmakers or public opinion to support or oppose a particular issue or cause.) The NRA was founded in 1871 to promote sport shooting, hunting, and firearm safety. The organization was not particularly successful in the late 1800s, but it benefited greatly from the Militia Act of 1903. This act created the National Board for the Promotion of Rifle Practice, which then authorized the inexpensive sale of surplus government weapons and ammunition to rifle clubs. In 1910, Congress allowed the U.S. military to simply give away extra guns to NRA-sponsored clubs. In 1912, the government began funding NRA shooting matches.

The NRA's cozy relationship with the government and the army helped it survive, but in 1921, the organization still had only about 3,500 members. By affiliating with thousands of local sporting clubs, the NRA saw its membership climb steadily until it boasted 50,000 members at the start of World War II in 1939. By 1948, as soldiers returning from the war showed an interest in guns, target shooting, and hunting, membership had tripled.

The NRA as an Advocacy Organization

The NRA focused on marksmanship and other sporting activities, but it has actively lobbied on gun control issues since the 1920s. In the 1920s and 1930s, the NRA accepted gun control laws in principle but opposed anything resembling national gun registration. The NRA wrote model legislation that was adopted by many states, establishing a permit system to carry concealed weapons. It also worked with the Justice Department to craft the Federal Firearms Act of 1938. In 1968, NRA executive vice president Franklin Orth testified on behalf of some aspects of the Gun Control Act. "We do not think," he

Since the mid-1970s, the NRA has held a more hard-line position on gun control than it did for the first hundred years of its existence, namely that gun control of any kind infringes on the rights granted to the people by the Constitution. The former president of the NRA, actor Charlton Heston, is pictured in 1999.

said, "that any sane American, who calls himself an American, can object to placing into this bill the instrument which killed the president of the United States [John F. Kennedy]." In the 1960s and early 1970s, the NRA actually supported a ban on the cheap handguns known as Saturday night specials. As Orth noted in the March 1968 issue of *American Rifleman,* the NRA "has been in support of workable, enforceable gun control legislation since its very inception in 1871."

This position changed in the mid-1970s, when hard-liners took control of the NRA and made opposition to any and all gun control a basic principle of the organization. Since then, the NRA has devoted a great deal of effort and resources to fighting all gun control legislation. In 1975, the NRA created the Institute for Legislative Action (ILA) to focus specifically on influencing political elections. In 1992, the ILA spent almost $30 million on political activities. To support its political campaigns, the NRA relies heavily on an individualist view of the Second Amendment, arguing that almost all gun control is an infringement of an individual's right to bear arms guaranteed by the Second Amendment.

By the mid-1970s, NRA membership reached 1 million, and it peaked at almost 3.5 million in the mid-1990s. In 1995, the organization's annual budget was about $150 million, a good part of which came from membership dues. In 1995, the NRA maintained a staff of 300 employees, including more than fifty specifically assigned to lobbying efforts. The organization is sometimes considered the best single-issue advocacy organization in the United States. The NRA boasts a large number of highly motivated members brought together by a common interest, willing to write letters, contribute money, attend meetings, and pressure politicians.

FAST FACT

Over the doors to the NRA headquarters are the words from the last half of the Second Amendment: "The Right of the People to Keep and Bear Arms, Shall Not Be Infringed." There's no mention of the first half of the amendment, which reads, "A well regulated militia, being necessary to the security of a free State..."

Other Anti–Gun Control Advocacy Organizations

The successes of the civil rights movement in the 1950s and 1960s spurred the growth of single-interest advocacy on topics such as abortion, school prayer, civil rights, and the death penalty. Groups that lobby for these interests maintain a narrow, intense focus on one specific issue; many members view the issue in fundamental moral terms of good (their side) and evil (the other side). Single-issue advocacy groups often rely on grassroots activism and winning over public opinion to their side.

Several anti–gun control organizations have formed since 1970, sometimes with direct or indirect help from the NRA. The connection between them all is the view that the Second Amendment protects an individual's right to own weapons. The Citizen's Committee for the Right to Keep and Bear Arms was formed in 1971 by gun enthusiasts who felt that the NRA was not active enough in opposing gun control laws. The Citizen's Committee also spun off another active organization, the Second Amendment Foundation (SAF).

The Gun Owners of America (GOA), formed in 1975, promotes itself as "the only no-compromise gun lobby in Washington." The GOA, which is smaller and more radical than the NRA, claims that its mission is "to preserve and defend the Second Amendment rights of gun owners. GOA sees firearms ownership as a freedom issue." The GOA sometimes claims that the Second Amendment grants Americans the right of revolution against the government. The NRA, the GOA, and the Citizen's Committee all played a role in the lobbying that resulted in the weakening of the Gun Control Act of 1968.

The Political Parties and Gun Control

In trying to win moderate voters, the national Democratic and Republican parties often avoid any meaningful disagreement with each other. Yet they have consistently disagreed over the value of gun control. The gun issue first appeared in party platforms in 1968, reflecting the chaos of the 1960s and the passage of the Gun Control Act. Since that time, the Democratic Party has generally backed gun regulation, while the Republican Party has supported individual gun ownership free of government control.

The Democratic Party platform of 1972 called for "laws to control the improper use of hand guns" and recommended a ban on cheap handguns. The Democratic Party continued to support popular gun control measures in all presidential elections through 2000. This is consistent with the party's general belief in government regulation.

The Republican Party platform of 1976 simply stated, "We support the right of citizens to keep and bear arms."

Michael Burns, president of a group called Handgun Control, Inc. (HCI), speaks to other gun-control advocates at a meeting in Charlotte, North Carolina, in 1999. The group met to express its views a few blocks away from where the NRA, criticized by the poster next to Burns, was holding its annual meeting.

In 1980, that wording was repeated with an added phrase urging removal of "those provisions of the Gun Control Act of 1968 that do not significantly impact on crime but serve rather to restrain the law abiding citizen in his legitimate use of firearms." After Ronald Reagan was elected president in 1980, the ideas in this sentence would be put into action in the Firearms Owners Protection Act of 1986. Reagan was the first president to attend an NRA convention, in 1983, where he promised to support the NRA's agenda: "[We] will never disarm any American who seeks to protect his or her family from fear or harm."

Despite the disagreement of the political parties, gun control is far from a party-line issue. In most gun control votes, the breakdown is often more by region than by party. The strongest opposition to gun control comes from Southern, Western, and rural representatives, regardless of party, while the strongest support usually comes from urban politicians, especially in the Northeast.

Backlash Against the Gun Control Act of 1968

FAST FACT

In 1981, John Hinckley Jr. used a cheap handgun to shoot President Ronald Reagan, but this brush with death did not affect Reagan's continued opposition to gun control of almost any kind.

In the election of 1980, the Republican Party won control of both the presidency and the Senate. Ronald Reagan's election signaled a major shift in American politics. The conservatives' "Republican revolution" claimed that the United States had gone wrong in the 1960s, and it was their mission to fix it. In foreign policy, Reagan's support for large defense budgets reminded Americans of the importance of weaponry to U.S. interests. Many Republicans opposed the Gun Control Act of 1968 as an example of a misguided, ineffective, and unconstitutional policy, and they set out to weaken it.

Attacks on the Gun Control Act of 1968 had started almost immediately after its passage. The very next year, Congress repealed a part of the act that required sellers of shotgun and rifle ammunition to register purchasers. In 1978, a subcommittee of Congress cut $4.2 million from the budget of the Bureau of Alcohol, Tobacco, and Firearms (BATF), halting an attempt to computerize its records to make it easier to trace guns. The subcommittee specifically stated, "No funds...shall be available for salaries or administrative expense in connection with consolidating or centralizing, within the Department of the Treasury, the records, or any portion thereof, of acquisition and disposition of firearms maintained by Federal firearms licensees."

The Firearms Owners Protection Act of 1986

The backlash against the Gun Control Act of 1968 climaxed with the passage of the Firearms Owners Protection Act on May 19, 1986. This act had a huge effect on the Gun Control Act by reinstating the interstate sale of rifles and shotguns and abolishing record-keeping requirements for ammunition dealers.

Republican senator James McClure of Idaho and Democratic representative Harold Volkmer of Missouri sponsored the Firearms Owners Protection Act, sometimes known as the McClure-Volkmer Act. The act began with a section of "Congressional Findings" that concluded that "the rights of citizens to keep and bear arms under the second amendment to the United States Constitution... required additional legislation to correct existing firearms statutes and enforcement policies."

The Firearms Owners Protection Act did away with much of the Gun Control Act of 1968 by weakening the government's ability to enforce the law and giving more power to the states. It drastically decreased penalties for violations by weapons dealers in preparing their paperwork. It also provided for the legal transportation by interstate travelers of "unloaded and inaccessible" guns, regardless of local restrictions. The act repealed federal restrictions on ammunition sales and out-of-state sales of rifles and shotguns.

Supporters of the Firearms Owners Protection Act argued that restrictions on interstate sales of guns and extended waiting periods to buy guns had no effect on crime-fighting, but instead were unjustified and unconstitutional limitations on sportsmen, hunters, and gun dealers. This law represented the high point of NRA influence in Washington, D.C., and the temporary triumph of anti-gun control forces.

Cop-Killer Bullets

Armor-piercing KTW bullets (named after the inventors, Paul Kopsch, Daniel Turcos, and Donald Ward) had been developed in the 1970s for use by law enforcement. Unfortunately, police departments found them ineffective because of their inaccuracy. However, KTW bullets could be used by criminals to pierce the bulletproof vests worn by the police. In the early 1980s, many law enforcement organizations joined together to try to have these "cop-killer bullets" banned.

Gun control opponents fought this effort for four years, again claiming that the Second Amendment prohibited any kind of gun control. They noted that there were no documented cases of police officers being killed by such bullets. Although the bullets had absolutely no hunting or sporting purposes, the NRA declared that the prohibition of cop-killer bullets was unconstitutional and part of a plot to take away legitimate gun rights. This extremely unpopular stance angered many police organizations, whose support the NRA needed in its lobbying for the Firearms Owners Protection Act. In 1986, the NRA finally withdrew its opposition, but the organization's relationship with law enforcement agencies and police organizations never entirely healed.

The Law Enforcement Officers Protection Act of 1986 banned the sale, manufacture, or import of armor-piercing ammunition, except in very limited circumstances. These types of ammunition were defined as any "that may be used in a handgun, and that are made of such metals as tungsten alloys, steel, brass, bronze, iron, beryllium, copper, or depleted uranium." The act declared mandatory five-year sentences for violations of the law. Although largely a symbolic victory, it represented a turning of the tide toward more national gun control legislation.

The Brady Campaign to Prevent Gun Violence

In the late 1980s and early 1990s, gun control advocates began to press their case for stronger national laws with greater effectiveness and skill. Imitation is said to be the sincerest form of flattery, and gun control organizations began to mimic the lobbying and organizational tactics that worked so well for the NRA.

The gun control movement gained ground after a series of bloody shootings that horrified the nation. In 1989, a gunman opened fire on a crowded schoolyard at Cleveland Elementary School in Stockton, California. He used a Chinese-made AK-47 assault rifle (purchased in

Oregon) fitted with a magazine holding seventy-five bullets (purchased in Rhode Island). A firearm's *magazine* is where the bullets are held before they pass into the gun chamber for firing. Firing off 105 rounds (he had more than one magazine), the gunman killed five students and wounded thirty-three others; he then killed himself. Two years later, a man killed twenty-two people (and then himself) and wounded twenty-three others in a cafeteria in Killeen, Texas. It was the worst such massacre in American history to that date.

Handgun Control, Inc. (HCI), had been formed in 1974 as the National Council to Control Handguns. It was the first and largest single-interest organization dedicated to gun control, especially regarding handguns. HCI gained many new members in 1980 after the murder of musician John Lennon by a killer with a cheap handgun. By 1981, the organization had 100,000 members.

In the 1980s and 1990s, HCI continued to grow under the leadership of Sarah Brady, the wife of James Brady, a White House press secretary who had been seriously

In 1997, former White House press secretary James Brady demonstrates a trigger lock at a press conference calling for child safety locks to be added to guns. Brady and his wife, Sarah, have been working for gun control since the 1981 assassination attempt on President Ronald Reagan that left James Brady seriously injured.

wounded in the 1981 attempt to assassinate President Ronald Reagan. A daughter of a Federal Bureau of Investigation (FBI) agent and a lifelong Republican, she joined HCI when it became apparent that the Republican Party would sponsor and support the Firearms Protection Act of 1986 to weaken gun control laws.

Under Brady's leadership, HCI membership reached 250,000 in 1990. In 1998, it reported membership of 400,000, and its annual budget topped $7 million. The organization specifically seeks to counter the power of the NRA by matching the amount of money that the NRA spends supporting political candidates, lobbying, and using the mass media to spread the HCI message. In 2000, however, HCI's resources were still only about one-tenth of the size of the NRA's. In June 2001, twenty years after James Brady was shot, HCI was renamed the Brady Campaign to Prevent Gun Violence.

HCI had begun in partnership with another gun control organization, the National Coalition to Ban Handguns (NCBH), formed at about the same time. The two groups soon parted ways. The NCBH, renamed the Coalition to Stop Gun Violence (CSGV) in 1990, is a group of more than forty religious, labor, medical, educational, and civic organizations, claiming 100,000 supporters. It takes a slightly tougher stand on gun regulation than the larger Brady Campaign, supporting stricter bans on handguns and assault-style weapons while claiming that "hunting weapons, such as shotguns and rifles, would be unaffected."

Waiting Periods

From 1987 to 1993, gun control proponents led by HCI fought for the passage of a national waiting period for handgun purchases. The waiting period had two purposes. It would serve as a cooling-off period for someone who wanted to buy and use a handgun on an angry impulse that he (most handgun owners are male) might not feel a week later. Secondly, it would give police departments or the government a chance to perform a background check in order to prevent the sale of firearms to potentially dangerous people such as ex-felons or the mentally disabled.

Gun control supporters' sponsorship of a waiting period for gun purchases was a clever public relations strategy. A waiting period represented a small degree of government regulation. It didn't forbid anyone from owning a handgun, rarely used in hunting anyway, but merely postponed the purchase a few days. At the same time, a waiting period would help deny guns to people who almost everyone agreed should not have them. Even people who believed that the Second Amendment protected an individual right to bear arms had trouble explaining how waiting periods would infringe on this right.

FAST FACT

The idea of a waiting period dated back to at least the 1930s, when a forty-eight-hour waiting period was put into use in Washington, D.C. The drafting of that rule was actually supported by the NRA, which continued to accept the idea in some form until the 1970s, when it reversed its position.

Ohio senator Howard Metzenbaum and Ohio representative Edward Feighan introduced the idea of a national waiting period in Congress in 1987. Despite this modest step, the proposal was the subject of enormous debate and intensive, expensive lobbying by both sides. The passage of a national waiting period became the top priority of HCI; correspondingly, the NRA claimed that a waiting period would not stop criminals from getting guns, that it inconvenienced those entitled to guns, and that it was the first step on a slippery slope to much stronger gun regulations. "Indeed," stated one NRA letter to its members, "hearing Congress rant and rave about gun control in recent weeks was enough to make any freedom-loving American sick."

The Brady Handgun Violence Protection Act of 1993

From 1988 to 1993, Congress voted on the Brady Handgun Violence Prevention Act eight times—five in favor; three against. After considerable political wrangling and compromise, Congress eventually passed the Brady Bill (as it was known) by a vote of 238 to 189 in the House and 63 to 36 in the Senate.

On November 30, 1993, President Bill Clinton signed the Brady Bill. It required a waiting period of five days to

On November 30, 1993, President Bill Clinton signed the Brady Bill into law. The law put several restrictions on the sale and purchase of handguns, including a five-day waiting period from the time a person first seeks to buy a handgun. James Brady sits next to the president.

purchase a handgun. It also charged the chief local law enforcement officials, such as county sheriffs, to make "a reasonable effort" to conduct background checks on people seeking to purchase weapons. Police would only have to do these background checks for five years, after which a computerized system would be used to conduct background checks instantly. The bill provided $200 million per year to help states upgrade their computerized records to make this system work. Titles II and III of the Brady Bill involved reporting requirements for multiple sales of handguns and thefts from dealers. License fees were increased from $30 to $200 for the first three years and cost $90 for renewals. The Brady Bill also made it a federal crime to steal firearms from licensed dealers.

Under the Brady Bill, about 6,600 handgun applications a month were rejected because the would-be purchasers fell into one of several forbidden categories, such as felons or drug users. In addition, the increase in license fees for gun dealers decreased the number of dealers from 285,000 before the law to 103,000 in 1996. Many of the dealers who disappeared did not have a physical store but were selling guns through the mail or over the Internet.

The NRA challenged the constitutionality of the Brady Bill, but not as a violation of the Second Amendment. Instead, it argued that the bill contradicted the Tenth Amendment, which protected the rights of states. In 1997, in the case of *Printz v. United States,* the U.S. Supreme Court agreed and struck down the part of the Brady Bill requiring local law enforcement authorities to conduct the checks. The actual impact of this ruling was very small, since on November 30, 1998, under terms of the law, the five-day waiting period was replaced by the national system of instant background checks.

The Assault Weapons Ban of 1994

Those favoring gun control successfully supported a national ban on assault weapons in 1994. *Assault-style semiautomatic weapons* are weapons that look more like military guns than civilian ones. *Semiautomatic* means that the gun fires one round each time that the trigger is squeezed, as opposed to a *fully automatic gun,* which fires many rounds with each trigger pull. (Fully automatic guns were already largely banned by 1994.) Assault weapons are almost never used for hunting and rarely used for self-defense.

FAST FACT

Gun magazines do not have serial numbers, so it was almost impossible for the government to prove that any particular magazine had been purchased after the 1994 ban on assault weapons was passed.

After the Stockton school massacre, President George H.W. Bush had immediately reversed his opposition to assault weapons regulations and banned the import of certain weapons by presidential order in March 1989. Bans of this type were continued by executive order through the Clinton administration, but it proved very difficult to get the legislation passed in Congress. In the next five years, some type of assault weapons ban was submitted to a vote six times in the Senate and six times in the House. Critics complained that the ban on assault weapons was purely symbolic politics that would have no effect on crime. Supporters claimed that assault weapons had a definite appeal to criminals and that a ban wouldn't hurt anyone with lawful intentions.

After angry debate, the ban on assault weapons finally passed Congress as part of the Omnibus Violent Crime Control and Law Enforcement Act of 1994. It prohibited for ten years the sale and possession of nineteen types of assault-style weapons, including several dozen copycat models that fell into the same category. The bill also limited magazine capacity to ten rounds. It specifically exempted more than 600 sporting rifles, as well as all guns and magazines owned legally before the law took effect.

The Second Amendment and Gun Control

The Second Amendment, regardless of how it is interpreted, did not prevent the passage of a host of gun control laws between 1963 and 1994. Popular opinion and the lobbying of anti-gun control organizations were far more effective than the Constitution in preventing the stricter regulation of firearms. The debate in this period was less over the inalienable right to keep and bear arms than over what kind of weapons the framers of the Constitution and the Bill of Rights would have consented to prohibit.

In general, opponents of gun control were more successful than gun control supporters in the political arena in this period. Americans who believed that the Second Amendment protected the individual right to bear arms succeeded in weakening the Gun Control Act of 1968 by passing the Firearms Owners Protection Act of 1986. Bans on assault weapons and cop-killer bullets were largely symbolic in nature. In the 1990s, gun control supporters were forced to claim the Brady Bill's simple five-day waiting period as an enormous victory.

The success of anti-gun control forces led some extremists to claim that the Second Amendment protected not only the individual right of gun ownership for self-defense, but also the right of Americans to use weapons in an armed revolt against a tyrannical government. The battles over the interpretation of the Second Amendment would become even more controversial in the 1990s.

CHAPTER 5

The Modern Debate over the Second Amendment

The Constitution rarely defines the freedoms that it protects, and this is especially true of the brief Bill of Rights. The meanings of the terms "freedom of speech" and "freedom of religion" (First Amendment), "unreasonable search and seizure" (Fourth Amendment), and "due process of law" (Fifth and Fourteenth Amendments) have been debated for more than 200 years, since the Constitution was ratified. Arguments over the meaning of the Second Amendment were infrequent in the 1800s and early 1900s, but in the last fifty years, this amendment has become the center of a controversial debate about the meaning of freedom and the Constitution.

Questions about the Second Amendment usually arise in debates over gun control. Some claim that the Second Amendment guarantees the right to have any weapon, while others want severe restrictions on firearms. To claim the right to its fullest extent—for example, to say that the Second Amendment protects the right to own nuclear weapons—actually weakens the argument, since few Americans will be sympathetic to their neighbors' right to have missiles in their backyards. Nonetheless, the Constitution is the highest law of the land and must be obeyed. Interpretations of the Second Amendment can be broken down into two general categories: "to keep and bear arms" as a collective right or as an individual right.

A Collective Right

Supporters of gun ownership as a collective right believe that the records of the Constitutional Convention of 1787 and the discussions about the Bill of Rights in Congress demonstrate that writers of the Second Amendment were specifically tying the keeping and bearing of arms to service in the militia. They believe that the meaning of the Second Amendment is very obvious if the words aren't twisted: that Congress may not make laws against the right of the people through their individual states to organize militias of arms-bearing citizens. Collectivists claim that the framers' only concern was with the concentration of military power in the hands of the federal government and that the Second Amendment was intended simply to guarantee that state militias would be maintained against a possible standing national army. That's why the Second Amendment begins with the phrase "A well regulated militia, being necessary to the security of a free State..."

Collective rights supporters argue that the Second Amendment does not give a private individual a constitutional right to keep and bear arms, because that question did not come up in the 1780s. At the Philadelphia convention, there was almost no reference to hunting, target shooting, dueling, personal self-defense, or any subject that would imply an individual right to have guns. There was also nothing in the pamphlets, newspapers, or debates of the time. Every reference to the right to keep and bear arms was in connection with military service.

Collectivists argue that the militia was an institution defined by the Constitution and then by Congress. Militias could not exist outside government regulation,

Those who support the view that gun ownership is a collective right claim that the framers of the Constitution were referring to the right to bear arms in the context of military service only—and in the 1700s, that meant militias. This illustration dramatizes the minutemen of the colonial period—ready to fight at a moment's notice.

and they were given the specific job to crush insurrections, which they had always done. Citizens do have the natural right of armed revolution against a dictatorship, but that is a right outside of American constitutional government. A person can't carry out a right of armed revolution against the American government while at the same time claiming protections from the U.S. Constitution. War against the United States is treason according to Article III, Section 3 of the Constitution.

Some collective rights supporters also argue that even if the Second Amendment does protect an individual right to gun ownership, it protects Americans only against laws by the national government and not by the states. In addition, the freedoms in the Bill of Rights are not absolute; freedom of religion, for example, cannot involve human sacrifice, and with or without the Second Amendment, gun ownership can still be regulated in the interest of public safety.

An Individual Right

Supporters of gun ownership as an individual right believe that the initial militia clause in the Second Amendment should be understood as simply helping to explain, and not restrict, the meaning of "to keep and bear arms." That is, while maintaining a "well regulated militia" was a major reason for including the Second Amendment in the Bill of Rights, it should not be viewed as the only reason. Other reasons, such as a right to individual self-defense, were implied in the Second Amendment. In this view, the individual citizen is guaranteed the right to own a weapon for self-defense and to use it against a government that may want to take his or her rights away. Common law has long permitted self-defense against threats to personal or family safety or property, and gun ownership is simply an extension of that right. If the question of gun ownership did not come up at the Constitutional Convention, it's because most Americans assumed a right to own and use firearms in the 1780s; no specific guarantees were necessary.

Second Amendment individualists insist that even if the presence of millions of guns causes some social problems, this is a small price to pay for a basic human freedom. They argue that many of the freedoms guaranteed by the Bill of Rights, such as the rights of the accused, often allow the guilty to go free for the sake of protecting the rights of the innocent. In the same way, high rates of gun-related homicides and accidental shootings are unfortunate, but like freedom of speech for a group whose ideas are distasteful to others, they are the by-product of living in a free society. Individual rights supporters also argue that guns serve a positive social function by allowing the weak to protect themselves, thereby holding down crime.

Some individualists also argue that the framers of the Constitution intended a militia to consist of all the people—the entire body of American citizens. If the right of "the people" to join a militia included all able-bodied white men (age eighteen to forty-five) in the eighteenth century, this right would, after passage of the Thirteenth Amendment (ending slavery), Fourteenth Amendment (giving citizenship to all native-born Americans), and Nineteenth Amendment (giving women the vote), now belong to everyone. Armed citizens not only fulfill the individual's natural right of self-defense, but also prevent oppression by the government. Even if Americans no longer depend on militias for national defense, their theoretical function remains crucial.

The Right of Revolution and the Second Amendment

Some people claim that Americans have a right to engage in rebellion or insurrection against the U.S. government if they believe it to be oppressive. This "right of revolution" is a way to make sure that the country's rulers listen to its citizens. Just as the American patriots had formed what they believed to be legal political organizations and militias in the 1770s to fight for their independence when they thought the British were abusing them, so Americans today keep the same right.

Followers of this theory claim that the Second Amendment protects this right to revolution. Article I, Section 8, of the Constitution seemed to have settled this question by stating that the definition of a militia would be decided by Congress. The individual rights interpretation, however, insists that the constitutionally protected "militia" is not an organized military force of the states but must be identified with the whole body of the people. Individualists claim that the militia should provide the last check on the tyrannical power of both state and federal government. Only well-armed people, possessing privately held weapons, can discourage would-be oppressors. If the Second Amendment is designed to allow people to resist governmental tyranny, then the right to bear arms would include military weapons such as artillery needed to combat the U.S. Army. This general militia would have to exist independently of the government or it couldn't protect the citizens against a dictatorship by that government or its army.

Opponents of this view note that the Constitution gives Congress the power to "provide for calling forth the Militia to execute the Laws of the Union, suppress insurrections and repel invasions." At the Virginia ratifying convention in June 1788, James Madison clearly stated that the militias were to be used to put down insurrections:

> [If] insurrections should arise, or invasions take place, the people ought unquestionably to be employed to suppress and repel them, rather than a standing army. The best way to do these things was to put the militia on a good and sure footing, and enable the government to make use of their services when necessary.

The Constitution nowhere endorses the right of revolution against republican government with free elections, but in fact specifically gives the national government the power to suppress by force anything even vaguely resembling revolution (such as the Whiskey Rebellion in 1794).

Thousands of people demonstrated in Tiananmen Square in Beijing, China, in the spring of 1989, calling for democratic reforms to China's Communist government. The government responded by crushing the rebellion, killing hundreds. This response led some people to question the possibility of a similar government reponse in the United States.

Still, what if the unthinkable happened and the United States did become a dictatorship? Although James Madison considered the possibility ridiculous in *The Federalist Papers,* he had at least considered the question. How would Americans be able to fight for freedom without weapons? An armed militia couldn't prevent governmental tyranny if it was organized and regulated by the power of the government. Americans had watched in horror as the People's Republic of China crushed the pro-democracy movement with tanks at Tiananmen Square in 1989. Individualists say that if such a thing happened in the United States, only an armed and involved citizenry could save the country.

The Incident at Ruby Ridge

Ruby Ridge, Idaho, was the mountain home of Randy Weaver, a white supremacist who had agreed to buy sawed-off shotguns from someone who turned out to be an undercover agent of the Bureau of Alcohol, Tobacco, and Firearms (BATF). On August 21, 1992, federal marshals surrounded Weaver's isolated cabin, planning to arrest him on weapons charges. A gun battle broke out after Weaver's dog alerted his family. Weaver's fourteen-year-old son, Sammy, was shot in the back and U.S. Marshal William Degan was also killed. The next day, although no one in Weaver's cabin had fired another shot and the federal marshals had given no warnings or demands to surrender, a Federal Bureau of Investigation (FBI) sniper killed Weaver's wife, Vicki, as she stood behind a cabin door holding her ten-month-old daughter.

The director of BATF compares a regular shotgun (left) and a sawed-off shotgun (right) during the hearings on the disastrous 1992 raid of Randy Weaver's property at Ruby Ridge, Idaho, by federal marshals and the FBI.

A criminal investigation outraged many Americans when it revealed that FBI agents had covered up evidence of "shoot on sight" orders. Weapons charges against Weaver were dismissed on the grounds that the FBI had entrapped, or tricked, him. The Justice Department's own report recommended criminal prosecution of federal agents, and the government agreed to pay Weaver and his surviving three daughters $3.1 million in compensation. In September 1995, the U.S. Senate held hearings on the Ruby Ridge incident. Its report, released in December, criticized the FBI and other law enforcement agencies for their actions in the incident.

The Incident at Waco

A Christian religious cult known as the Branch Davidians, headed by David Koresh, had its main headquarters outside of Waco, Texas. On February 28, 1993, the BATF raided the compound in order to serve arrest and search warrants as part of an investigation into illegal possession of firearms and explosives located there.

A gunfight broke out between federal officers and Branch Davidians (it is in dispute who fired the first shot). Four BATF agents were killed and twenty wounded in the first assault on the compound. This led to a two-month siege of the building. U.S. attorney general Janet Reno claimed that Koresh was abusing children in the compound (also in dispute), a criminal act that required an end to the standoff. In May, the United States launched a tear-gas attack, and parts of the compound caught fire. Eighty members of the Branch Davidians sect died. Later reports sharply criticized the BATF for mishandling the raid and then lying to cover up its mistakes.

Many Americans, even those unsympathetic to David Koresh or the Branch Davidians, were outraged by such a heavy-handed government response. An extremist minority saw in the Waco and Ruby Ridge incidents the beginning of a governmental dictatorship in the United States and vowed to stop it, with weapons if necessary.

The New Militia Movement

In the early 1990s, self-appointed "militias" began to form in the United States. These organizations are heavily armed, mainly male, and typically rural, many of them located in Western states. The new militias mix together white supremacists, gun-control opponents, survivalists, and Christian cultists. The connection between these different groups is total opposition to government involvement in the daily lives of U.S. citizens. The members of these new militias refer to themselves as "patriots," drawing a clear connection between their organizations and the Americans who created the American Revolution against the British. They strongly believe in the insurrectionist theory of the Second Amendment, which supposedly gives Americans not only the right to own weapons, but also the right of revolution.

Events of the 1990s boosted the growth of the new militia movement. Many people were particularly enraged by the FBI siege at Ruby Ridge and the raid on the Branch Davidians' compound at Waco. New militia supporters also

The Branch Davidian compound near Waco, Texas, is engulfed in flames after a tear-gas attack by BATF agents. The agents' goal was to coax the cult's leader, David Koresh, out of the compound to face criminal charges. Instead, eighty people, including Koresh, were killed.

detest the Brady Bill handgun control legislation passed by Congress in 1993. New militia members view this as yet another step on the road to the disarming of the people and the creation of a dictatorship in the United States.

The Bureau of Alcohol, Tobacco, and Firearms

The idea leading to the Bureau of Alcohol, Tobacco, and Firearms (BATF) dates back to the days of the Whiskey Rebellion of 1794, when Alexander Hamilton's tax on whiskey had to be collected by some federal governmental organization. In 1919, the passage of the Eighteenth Amendment led to the creation of a Bureau of Prohibition under the Treasury Department. The unit became the Alcohol Tax Unit when Prohibition ended in 1933 and was renamed the Alcohol and Tobacco Tax Division in 1951, when it was assigned to collect taxes on tobacco.

FAST FACT

During the 1920s and 1930s, Elliot Ness was a nationally famous law officer who worked for the Bureau of Prohibition. His name became well known from the *Untouchables* television show and movie.

After the passage of federal gun laws in 1934 and 1938, the Alcohol and Tobacco Tax Division was given the responsibility of enforcing the law in 1942. As a result of the Gun Control Act of 1968, the agency was renamed the Bureau of Alcohol, Tobacco, and Firearms and assigned the duty of issuing licenses to firearms dealers and making sure they kept proper records. The BATF is in charge of all matters dealing with gun regulations, including licensing, tracing guns, and tracking illegal movement of firearms and explosives.

Gun control supporters argue that the BATF is a weak and relatively ineffective agency. For example, in 1985, the agency employed only 400 inspectors to monitor over 200,000 gun dealers; in 1994, about 250 agents monitored 280,000 gun dealers. But many gun control opponents claim that the BATF harasses honest gun owners and dealers for no reason and that there is insufficient check on its power.

"Jackbooted Fascists"

The insurrectionist theory of the Second Amendment thrives on antigovernment rhetoric that has become ever

FAST FACT

In the spring of 1995, the NRA's executive vice president, Wayne LaPierre, wrote in a fund-raising letter that a ban on assault weapons gave "jackbooted government thugs more power to take away our constitutional rights." Former president George H.W. Bush was so offended that he immediately sent a letter resigning his membership in the NRA, calling LaPierre's letter a "vicious slander on good people."

stronger since the 1980s. President Ronald Reagan famously said, "Government is not the solution to our problem, government is the problem." In 1981, a movie produced by the NRA, called *It Can Happen Here,* depicted BATF agents as Nazis oppressing honest citizens. (The Nazis in Germany murdered millions of people during World War II.) Nonetheless, proposals to abolish the BATF and assign its duties to the U.S. Secret Service—the law enforcement division of the Department of the Treasury—were opposed by the NRA. Gun advocacy groups, despite their criticism of the BATF, much prefer that gun control be in the hands of that weak and underfunded organization than placed with a publicly respected and fully computerized agency.

Attacks on the BATF picked up speed in the early 1990s, especially after the botched raids at Ruby Ridge and Waco. Michigan's Democratic representative, John Dingell (also an NRA board member), claimed that BATF investigators were "jackbooted American fascists." (Jackboots were worn by the Nazis.)

Talk-radio shows also heaped contempt on the BATF, helping to create an environment where violence was considered acceptable. Extremist talk-show host G. Gordon Liddy (syndicated on more than 250 stations) had been convicted as a felon in the infamous Watergate burglary of 1973 that led to the resignation of President Richard Nixon. On August 26, 1994, Liddy told his listeners, "Now if the Bureau of Alcohol, Tobacco, and Firearms comes to disarm you and they are bearing arms, resist them with arms. Go for a head shot; they're going to be wearing bulletproof vests."

In 1994, Republicans won control of both the Senate and the House of Representatives for the first time in almost fifty years. Early in 1995, Senate majority leader Bob Dole of Kansas and Speaker of the House Newt Gingrich of Georgia both publicly pledged to make a repeal of the assault weapons ban a top priority.

The Oklahoma City Bombing

April 19, 1995, seemed no different from any other day in Oklahoma City. Federal employees came to work at the Alfred P. Murrah Federal Office Building downtown and parents dropped their children off at the day care center there. Shortly after nine o'clock in the morning, Timothy McVeigh parked a rental truck filled with explosives in front of the building, lit the fuses, and walked away. The massive bomb inside the truck exploded, destroying half of the nine-story building. For nearly two weeks, as a stunned and horrified nation watched, the bodies of 168 men, women, and children were pulled from the rubble (700 people were wounded). It was the worst terrorist attack on American soil until the attacks on September 11, 2001.

McVeigh and his ex-army buddy, Terry Nichols, were charged with the bombing. McVeigh was convicted in June 1997 and received the death penalty; he was executed on June 11, 2001—the first federal prisoner executed in the United States in thirty-eight years. In December, a jury

FAST FACT

Randy Weaver, survivor of the Ruby Ridge incident, said that it pained him to learn of McVeigh's motive. "Every time my name was mentioned, it bugged me.... I know how the parents of those kids feel. And the spouses."

Timothy McVeigh was convicted of the Oklahoma City bombing in 1995 and given the death penalty for his crime. He was executed in June 2001. McVeigh cited the incidents at Ruby Ridge and Waco as his motivation for mounting an attack on the federal government.

refused to convict Nichols of murder, instead finding him guilty of involuntary manslaughter and of conspiring with McVeigh; Nichols was sentenced to life imprisonment.

McVeigh told the authors of a book on the bombing that he carried out the attack as revenge for the 1992 U.S. government siege at Ruby Ridge and the 1993 federal action near Waco. The murders, especially those of the children in the day care center, focused national attention on self-appointed "militias."

From Insurrection to Crime Statistics

The Oklahoma City bombing abruptly ended (although probably only temporarily) the debate over the Second Amendment and the right to revolution. Although the people had died from a bomb made of fuel oil and fertilizer and not gunfire, public opinion turned completely against the antigovernment rhetoric that had accompanied efforts to weaken gun control laws. Intellectual supporters of the insurrectionist theory tried to disassociate themselves from the new militia movement that they had helped to create and legitimize.

Support for a repeal of the assault weapons ban was weakened when Senator Robert Dole became the Republican presidential candidate in 1996. He realized that a strong stand against the ban would probably hurt his chances in the election. A repeal of the ban passed the House in March 1996 by a 239 to 173 vote (not enough to override an expected veto from President Clinton) but it never came to a vote in the Senate. Since 1996, the debate over the Second Amendment has temporarily moved away from political theory to the more practical question of whether fewer guns or more guns is the most effective strategy to prevent crime.

The Decline in Crime

The new debate over the Second Amendment takes place against a stunning decline in crime, especially in homicides, in the United States. After peaking in 1991, the violent crime rate declined for the next decade, reaching thirty-year lows. In the 1950s, the national homicide rate had been below 5 per 100,000 people annually. However, in 1963, the homicide rate began climbing steadily, reaching 9.8 per 100,000 in 1974 and peaking at 10.2 in 1980. It stayed in that general range until 1993, when it began the sharp decline that has brought crime rates down to their lowest level in thirty years (6.3 in 1998). Although the chances of dying in a violent crime remain higher in the United States than in almost any other industrialized nation, the odds are decreasing and concentrated in certain portions of the population, such as African-Americans and the poor.

FAST FACT

Homicide rates are probably the only accurate crime statistics. Other crimes may or may not be reported, but murders almost always attract attention.

For example, the murder rate in Manhattan in New York City peaked at 661 for the year 1972. There were still 503 murders in Manhattan in 1990, but only 106 in 2000 and a miniscule 82 in 2002—the lowest number in more than a hundred years. In New York City as a whole, the number of homicides dropped from 2,245 in 1990 to 671 in 1999. Since New York has always had some of the strictest gun control laws in the nation, it's almost impossible to credit those laws for either the shocking rise in crime or its meteoric decline. Nonetheless, both sides in the gun control debate attempt to use the statistics to back their own positions.

The reasons for the historic decline in the crime rates are disputed. A variety of theories have been proposed: the improved economy, tougher sentencing, advances in information technology, better methods of policing. Supporters of gun control point to the Brady Bill and other gun control legislation passed in the late 1980s and early 1990s. Opponents of gun control note the increasing number of Americans who own guns and the many state laws that now permit the carrying of concealed weapons.

During these years of declining crime rates, American firearms legislation has become more permissive on the state level and stricter on the national level. With so many different national, state, city, and local laws relating to gun use, it's virtually impossible to draw any reasonable conclusions regarding the success or lack of success of gun control laws. Some areas have strict standards, some have no standards, and no area is really able to seal itself off from guns.

The Racial Question

For many varied reasons, an unusually large number of America's violent crimes are committed by African-Americans against African-Americans (statistically, blacks usually kill blacks and whites generally kill whites). In 1994, African-Americans were 12 percent of the American population but made up 56 percent of the people arrested for murder. Among black male teenagers, the gun death rate rose from 37 per 100,000 in 1985 to 100 in 1990. In 2000, after several years of a falling crime rate, the rate of gun deaths among black male teens was still 56 per 100,000; more than 1,300 black male teenagers were killed with guns that year.

Many African-Americans claim that gun control is really race control, a tool historically used by whites to disarm and oppress the black population of America. The Congress of Racial Equality (CORE), a famous black civil rights organization, opposed gun control laws in 2000, claiming that "they bear especially hard on the poor and minorities." Although noting that crime was "the scourge of black neighborhoods and the black community," CORE believed that gun ownership offered a reasonable form of self-defense. In this view, gun laws, like drug laws, were racist in their effects if not in their intent, because they were applied haphazardly by racist police officers against people that they simply didn't like.

The Decline of Hunting

The gradual decline of hunting has also shifted the debate on the Second Amendment from rifles to handguns. A recent survey by the U.S. Fish and Wildlife Service revealed a sharp decline in the popularity of hunting in the United States. Between 1996 and 2001, the number of hunters declined from 14 million to 13 million—a 7 percent decrease. Hunting is most popular among older men in rural areas; in 1991, 22 percent of the American population lived in rural areas but accounted for 46 percent of the nation's hunters. By 2001, the rural population had dropped to 19 percent and accounted for 41 percent of the nation's hunters.

As more children grow up in cities and suburbs, the area available to go hunting is decreasing, and people have to travel greater distances to hunt. Parents play a key role in passing on the hunting tradition, since it's less likely that people will take up a sport if they didn't try it as a child, yet fewer Americans are taking their children out into the woods to hunt. Many suburbanites are reluctant to take up a sport that they see as both dangerous and cruel.

FAST FACT

According to the International Hunter Education Association, somewhere between 1,000 and 1,800 hunters were shot by accident in the United States and Canada each year between 1987 and 1997.

The Impact of September 11, 2001, on Gun Use

The first reaction of some Americans after the horrific terrorist attacks of September 11, 2001, was to buy guns. Gun sales, concealed weapons permits, and background checks for weapons all rose sharply in the months following the attacks. One opponent of gun control noted,

> September 11 was a wake-up call to America that we are vulnerable to terrorists. Now politicians need to wake up and start repealing the 21,000 gun control laws they passed over the last few decades...[which] prevent Americans from protecting themselves and their families from murderous terrorists.

Congress moved to arm airline pilots, even against the wishes of many airline pilots themselves.

At the same time, after September 11, the antigovernment rhetoric that went hand-in-hand with most opposition to gun control sounded a little hollow. There was certainly less sympathy for the view that the government was the enemy; patriotism rose as people perceived the government as a friend fighting terrorism.

The Bush Administration's Change of Federal Policy

While Americans were willing to wait on longer lines for security checks at airports after September 11, there was no similar movement for a longer waiting period for gun purchases or a national firearms registry. At first, it seemed as if supporters of more government regulation would have the advantage, as U.S. attorney general John Ashcroft made it clear that the government would restrict some freedoms in order to combat terrorism. Presumably, an administration dedicated to fighting terrorism would be concerned about the easy access to firearms by potential terrorists. However, in November 2001, the U.S. Justice Department under Ashcroft issued a historic statement claiming that the U.S. government now believed that the Second Amendment "protects the gun ownership rights of individuals, including persons who are not members of the militia, to bear firearms." This new

A 1999 Texas survey found that whether they owned handguns or not, a majority of people agree that child safety locks on guns are a good idea. A gun shop owner in that state demonstrates an eight-dollar lock that can be added to a gun to ensure that it does not fire accidentally.

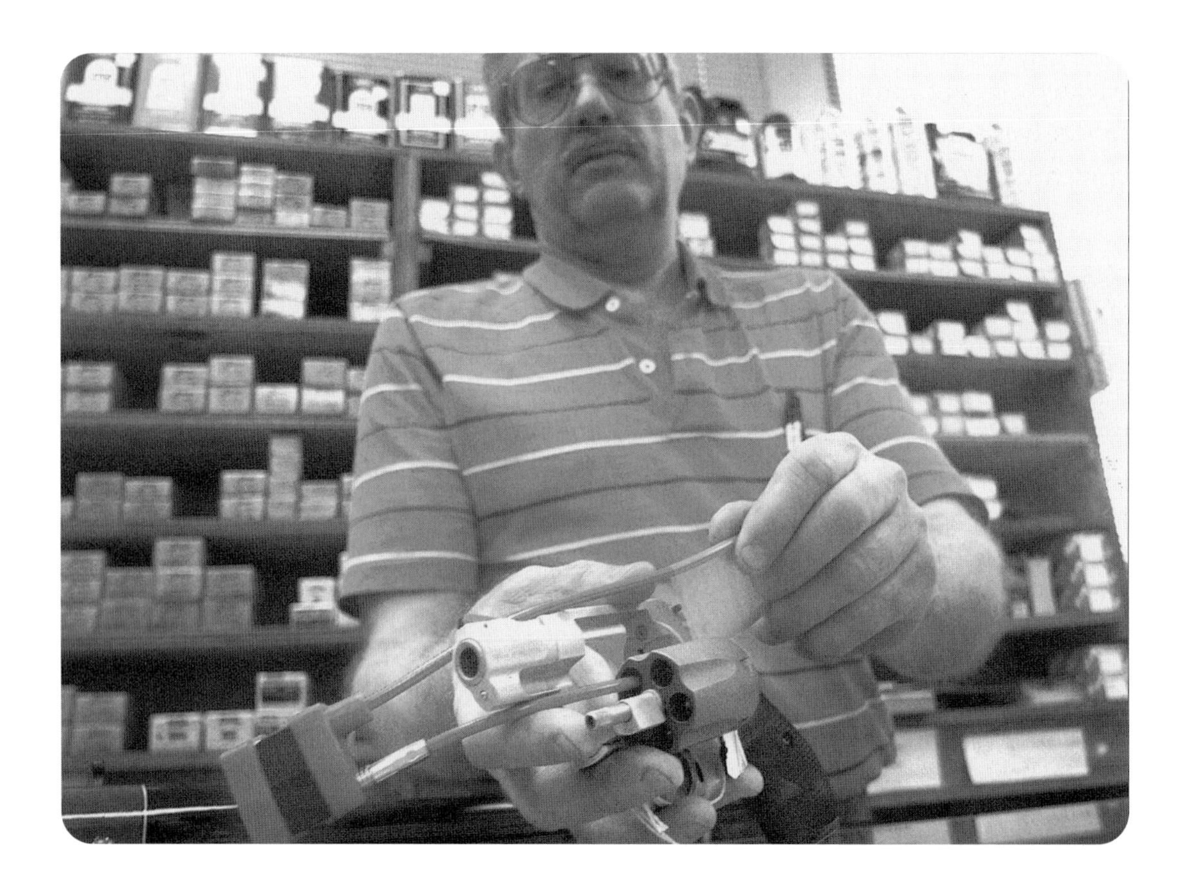

position reversed the government's interpretation of the Second Amendment that dated back more than half a century. The shift in government policy led immediately to several legal challenges to American gun laws.

The Cycle of Outrage

Interpretations of the Second Amendment often depend on sensational current events (or the lack of them). A horrible, highly publicized incident of gun violence leads to popular outrage. Gun control supporters press for stronger gun laws; anti–gun control forces launch counterattacks. Both sides cite the Second Amendment as proof that their cause is correct. This cycle of outrage, action, and reaction has become a regular feature of the American debate over the Second Amendment and gun control.

One example of this type of incident was the murder of Yoshihiro Hattori, a sixteen-year-old Japanese exchange student, near Baton Rouge, Louisiana, on Halloween night 1992. Hattori, costumed and looking for a party, mistakenly approached the door of the Pearis family. When he entered the family's carport to ask directions, Mr. Pearis ordered him to "freeze." When Hattori continued to advance, perhaps not understanding the command, Pearis shot and killed him with a revolver. Pearis was tried for manslaughter in 1993 but was acquitted on the grounds that he believed that he was facing a legitimate threat. Hattori's parents did win $660,000 in a civil action in September 1994. Supporters of gun control cited the Hattori incident as a tragic example of why further restrictions on gun ownership were necessary. Supporters of gun rights called the incident a freakish accident that shouldn't lead to wholesale changes in the nation's gun laws.

In 1997 and 1998, Americans were shocked by schoolyard shootings committed by school-aged boys in Jonesboro, Arkansas; Springfield, Oregon; Pearl, Mississippi; Edinboro, Pennsylvania; Johnston, Rhode Island; Pomona, California; Fayetteville, Tennessee; and

West Paducah, Kentucky. The sensational nature of these shootings hid the fact that the number of crimes committed on school grounds is relatively small and declining. Nonetheless, gun control supporters tried to use each well-publicized murder as a way to gain momentum for their cause.

The Weakness of the Gun Control Movement

FAST FACT

In 2003, director Michael Moore's movie in support of gun control, *Bowling for Columbine,* won an Oscar for best documentary.

After the 1999 massacre at Columbine High School in Colorado, the Clinton administration, joined by many in Congress, supported renewed gun control measures. The push seemed to have popular support, symbolized by the Million Mom March on Mother's Day (May 14) in 2000. Hundreds of thousands of mothers (and others) gathered in Washington, D.C., and elsewhere to urge lawmakers to pass stricter gun control laws.

There was particular interest in closing the so-called gun-show loophole in the Brady Bill. More than 4,000 gun shows are held in the United States every year, and an estimated 40 percent of gun sales occur at such gun shows, flea markets, or pawnshops. The Brady Bill, however, required only licensed gun dealers to perform background checks on customers purchasing firearms. All four of the guns used by the murderers in the Columbine High School massacre were acquired at gun shows from private sellers who did not perform background checks.

Despite the seeming support for gun control laws after the Columbine massacre, however, none of these measures was passed by Congress. With the Republican Party in control of both houses of Congress and the presidency from 2000 to 2004, stricter gun regulation as an issue seems dead—for the time being. It seems equally certain, however, that arguments over the meaning and application of the Second Amendment will remain part of American politics for a long time to come.

CHAPTER 6

The Judicial View of the Second Amendment

The Constitution of the United States may be the highest law of the land, but it is a short document. Its brevity has always raised questions about the meaning of some of its words. One of the weaknesses of the Articles of Confederation was the lack of a national court system to settle these disputes. Article III of the Constitution represents the framers' attempt to solve this problem by creating a national Supreme Court.

Although its powers are not well defined in the Constitution, most Americans agree that the Supreme Court should have the final say when there is an argument over the interpretation of the words of the Constitution. The U.S. Supreme Court usually hears cases only after they have been tried in lower local, state, or national courts. Since the Judiciary Act of 1869, the Supreme Court has been made up of nine members, known as *justices,* who vote to decide each legal case that they hear. A simple majority is enough to decide the case. Supreme Court justices are appointed for life so that public opinion or the need to be reelected will not sway them.

Common Law

Common law is the system of law used in England and in places like the United States that were colonized by England. The name dates back to the Middle Ages and the idea that the law of the English king's court represented the common custom everywhere in England. To some degree, self-defense has been an acceptable defense in the common-law tradition. Regardless of the interpretation of the Second Amendment, personal defense and defense of property are protected by law.

In the United States, the courts make common law when they decide cases. Unless there is a specific law that deals with an issue, the previous decisions of the courts (known as *precedents*) decide the case. This idea is represented by the Latin term *stare decisis,* or "let the decision stand." This means that the previous decisions of

Common law is the idea that what has gone before dictates the current law. If an issue is not governed by a specific law, then common law can be determined by the highest court that deals with the issue. Common law was first used in England. This illustration is of an English jury in the 1890s.

the highest court on the matter—for example, the Supreme Court in the United States—are binding in all other courts.

Police Power

In the antebellum era (1815–1860) before the U.S. Civil War, state legislatures began making laws on the assumption that they had a rightful interest in protecting the public's safety. When these laws were challenged, state and federal courts agreed that state governments possessed "police powers." State governments were permitted to override both individual and property rights to some degree in order to preserve public order and maintain minimum standards of health, safety, and welfare for the people they served. This police power was nowhere specifically spelled out but assumed to be a part of the reason for having a government in the first place.

In *Commonwealth v. Alger* in 1851, noted Massachusetts chief justice Lemuel Shaw stated that the state legislature could make "all manner of wholesome and reasonable laws... as they shall judge for the good of the commonwealth." According to Shaw, the rights of private property were not absolute but "subject to such reasonable limitations in their enjoyment" by legislatures. Supporters of gun laws in the United States almost always justified them by claiming this police power. This was not an unanswerable argument; their opponents would counter by taking an individual rights view of the Second Amendment.

Gun Law in the Nineteenth Century

Gun laws were common in the United States in the 1800s. Some of these laws were aimed at keeping weapons out of the hands of African-Americans, but many attempted to protect the public and maintain law and order. By the late 1800s, most American city governments had passed laws forbidding residents to carry concealed weapons or fire a gun in a public place. Some communities passed laws banning the public display of firearms unless the owner was hunting, taking the weapon for repair, or going to or from a militia meeting.

These laws were occasionally challenged as violations of the Second Amendment or similar clauses in state constitutions, but the courts rarely upheld these challenges. A typical response was an Alabama supreme court ruling of 1840 which noted in regard to the Second Amendment,

> A Statute, which, under pretense of *regulating* the manner of bearing arms...[renders] them wholly useless for the purpose of defense, would be clearly unconstitutional. But a law which is intended merely to promote personal security, and to put down lawless aggression and violence, and to that end inhibits the wearing of certain weapons...does not come in collision with the constitution.

Antebellum State Courts and Guns

The U.S. Supreme Court took a limited role in Bill of Rights cases before the Civil War. In the case of *Barron v. Baltimore* in 1833, the U.S. Supreme Court specifically ruled that the Bill of Rights protected citizens from abuses only by the national government, not by the states. Therefore, most cases involving gun regulations were heard by the state courts.

In the case of *Bliss v. Commonwealth* in 1822, Bliss wore a concealed weapon (a sword, not a gun) inside a cane in violation of a Kentucky law against carrying "concealed arms." The state court ruled that one of the amendments to the Kentucky constitution granted an individual the right to bear arms. The court stated that "in principle, there is no difference between the wearing [of] concealed arms, and a law forbidding the wearing such as are exposed." In addition, the right to bear arms "existed at the adoption of the constitution; it had then no limits short of the moral power of the citizens to exercise it and it in fact consisted in nothing else but in the liberty of the citizens to bear arms." This was one of the strongest state court assertions of an individual right to keep and bear arms. In 1850, the Kentucky legislature revised the state constitution to allow such legislation, adding a clause that "the general assembly may pass laws to prevent persons from carrying concealed firearms."

On the other hand, *Aymette v. State* in 1840 represented the strongest state court decision that an individual had a right to bear arms only if there was a public end in mind. In this case, a Tennessee state court considered whether the Second Amendment could prevent the state legislature from making a law forbidding any person from wearing a concealed bowie knife. The Tennessee court ruled that when the Constitution referred to a right to keep and bear arms, it was referring to those weapons that were "usually employed in civilized warfare, and constitute the ordinary military equipment." The court therefore accepted the Tennessee legislature's "right to prohibit the wearing, or keeping [of] weapons dangerous to the peace and safety of the citizens, and which are not used in civilized warfare, or would not contribute to the common defense." The Court also ruled that the phrase "to bear arms" referred to military use, not to individuals who wanted to carry concealed weapons for their own purposes. Although the right to bear arms must be respected, "it does not follow that the legislature is prohibited from passing laws regulating the manner in which these arms may be employed."

The Fourteenth Amendment and "Incorporation"

After the Civil War, most Americans realized that the Southern states, dominated by white racists, would never protect the rights of the recently freed slaves. The infamous Black Codes, passed by many of these states directly after the Civil War, virtually attempted to reenslave African-Americans.

As a result, Congress passed the Fourteenth Amendment to the Constitution, ratified by the necessary number of states in 1868. After the Bill of Rights, the Fourteenth Amendment is arguably the most important amendment in the Constitution. It contains large but vaguely defined checks on the power of states. The crucial Section 1 reads: "No State shall make or enforce any law which shall abridge the privileges or immunities of the citizens of the United States; nor shall any State deprive any person of life, liberty, or property, without due process of law; nor deny to any person within its jurisdiction the equal protection of the law."

The process of applying the Bill of Rights to the states by way of the Fourteenth Amendment is known as "incorporation." In a series of cases between 1920 and 1968, the U.S. Supreme Court interpreted the Fourteenth Amendment to include many parts of the Bill of Rights. State and local governments became bound by the same restrictions that had applied all along to the federal government. It is impossible to imagine the success of any civil rights movement, whether for African-Americans, women, the handicapped, Native Americans, or homosexuals, without the power of the Fourteenth Amendment.

However, not every part of the Bill of Rights has been officially applied to the states. When the U.S. Supreme Court has ruled on the Second Amendment, it has specifically refused to apply this amendment to the states. The last time that the Supreme Court subjected the Second Amendment to a detailed examination was in 1939 in the case of *United States v. Miller*. This case occurred before the civil rights revolution and the incorporation of most of the Bill of Rights to the states through the Fourteenth Amendment. Some people claim that in the light of the rulings of the civil rights era, Americans should simply assume that the Second Amendment applies to the states. Opponents note that the Supreme Court has never incorporated the Second Amendment despite many opportunities to do so. Since 1975, the trend of the U.S.

The Fourteenth Amendment to the Constitution, ratified in 1868, incorporated the restrictions of the Bill of Rights to the states; previously the Bill of Rights had applied only to the federal government. Since then, questions of how to interpret these rights as they apply to the states have continually been debated.

Supreme Court has been to refuse to incorporate any more of the Bill of Rights but instead to give the individual states more leeway in making their own laws. The issue of incorporation is crucial to the interpretation of the Second Amendment. Since it has not been incorporated, then regardless of its Constitutional protections, it does not apply to state or municipal gun control laws.

United States v. Cruikshank

After the Civil War, a racial war took place across much of the South to determine who would control the state governments. In Louisiana in 1873, an armed white force known as the White League killed more than 100 black men in the militia over a disputed election for governor. Three white men involved in this Colfax Massacre were found guilty of violating Section 6 of the Enforcement Act of 1870, which prohibited conspiracies from denying the constitutional rights of any citizen, including depriving African-Americans of their rights to own guns.

On March 27, 1876, in *United States v. Cruikshank,* the Supreme Court ruled in favor of the defendants by a vote of nine to nothing. According to the majority decision, written by Justice Morrison Waite, the right to assemble and to bear arms in the First and Second Amendments protected citizens only from federal congressional interference. Waite wrote,

> Bearing arms for a lawful purpose...is not a right granted by the Constitution.... The second amendment declares that it shall not be infringed; but this...means no more than that it shall not be infringed by Congress. This is one of the amendments that has no other effect than to restrict the powers of the national government.

At the time of this case, the U.S. Supreme Court was concerned with congressional efforts to broaden federal powers. The Supreme Court tried to put a quick end to this effort by ruling that the Fourteenth Amendment guarantees

More than a hundred blacks were killed by an armed white force in the Colfax Massacre in Louisiana in 1873. This illustration of the event was published in a contemporary magazine. The court decision that came as a result of the killings was influential in limiting the effectiveness of the Fourteenth Amendment.

of the right to due process and equal protection did not apply to violations by individuals. The court concluded that Louisiana could punish the offenses committed in the Colfax Massacre. Unfortunately, the likelihood that Southern states would prosecute racial terror by whites remained small for the next ninety years. This ruling greatly weakened the Fourteenth Amendment by completely denying it any power to incorporate the Bill of Rights.

Cruikshank has been attacked on many grounds as an outdated and racist decision. It left punishment in the hands of white racist juries in Louisiana and limited the federal government's ability to enforce its constitutional guarantees as stated in the Fourteenth Amendment. In regard to the Second Amendment, however, it established several principles that have never been overturned. In *Cruikshank*, the U.S. Supreme Court clearly accepted some regulation of firearms. In addition, the justices declared that the Second Amendment is not incorporated in the

Fourteenth Amendment, meaning that it restricts only the federal government and not the state government. Although most of the other freedoms in the first ten amendments have been incorporated by the Fourteenth Amendment to the states, the Supreme Court has not yet wavered from the decision in *Cruikshank* that the Second Amendment does not apply to the states.

Presser v. Illinois

In 1879, Herman Presser was indicted for violating an Illinois state law that prohibited parading with weapons by groups other than organized militia. He was convicted on the charge. Presser, who had been leading about 400 members of a fraternal organization armed with rifles in a parade through the Chicago streets, challenged the law on the grounds that it violated both his Second and Fourteenth Amendment rights. The U.S. Supreme Court's opinion in *Presser v. Illinois,* written by Justice William B. Woods, rejected Presser's claims by a nine to nothing vote on January 4, 1886. The court once again denied the incorporation of the Second Amendment, claiming that it limited action only by the federal government and citing the Cruikshank case by name.

Woods's opinion also noted that the Illinois law did not interfere with the right to keep and bear arms. State governments did not have the right to totally disarm their populations, because that would interfere with the federal government's ability to raise a militia from the population at large. Woods wrote that

> the States cannot...prohibit the people from keeping and bearing arms, so as to deprive the United States of their rightful resource for maintaining the public security, and disable the people from performing their duty to the General Government. But, as already stated, we think it is clear that the sections under consideration do not have this effect.

More importantly, the Supreme Court totally rejected the idea that citizens could form their own militias without the control of the state. Military organization and military drill under arms, according to the court, were "subjects especially under the control of the government of every country. They cannot be claimed as a right independent of law." This reaffirmed Congress's assignment by the Constitution to organize (and therefore define) militias.

The *Presser* case supported the view that the right to keep and bear arms in the Second Amendment could be understood only if it was connected to the first clause that dealt with the existence of the militia. A series of cases after *Presser* followed this general understanding of the Second Amendment. In 1894, the U.S. Supreme Court ruled in *Miller v. Texas* that a Texas law "prohibiting the carrying of dangerous weapons" did not violate the Second Amendment. In this case, the U.S. Supreme Court took the position that the restrictions of the Second Amendment "operate only upon the Federal power" and do not apply to the states.

United States v. Miller

The case of *United States v. Miller* was the last time that the Supreme Court specifically ruled on the issue of the meaning of the Second Amendment. In 1934, Jack Miller and Frank Layton were convicted of transporting an unregistered twelve-gauge sawed-off shotgun, having a barrel less than 18 inches (45 centimeters) long, across state lines in violation of the National Firearms Act of 1934. Miller challenged the act's constitutionality, claiming that it violated his Second Amendment rights. He also claimed that a national firearms act was an improper use of Congress's right to control interstate commerce. A lower court agreed.

In 1939, a unanimous Supreme Court decision reversed the lower ruling. The court stated that federal taxing power could be used to regulate guns. Therefore, firearm registration as presented in the National Firearms Act of 1934 was constitutional. The court also clearly stated that the Second Amendment must be interpreted by its "obvious purpose" of ensuring an effective militia. Justice James McReynolds, writing for the Court, declared,

> In the absence of any evidence tending to show that possession of a "shotgun having a barrel of less than eighteen inches in length" at this time has some reasonable relationship to the preservation or efficiency of a well-regulated militia, we cannot say that the Second Amendment guarantees the right to keep and bear such an instrument. Certainly it is not within judicial notice that this weapon is any part of the ordinary military equipment or that its use could contribute to the common defense.

The implication seemed to be that citizens could possess a constitutional right to keep and bear arms only in connection with service in a militia. If Congress or the states wanted to regulate firearms, it was within their power to do so. On the other hand, if military use was the decisive test (as the Supreme Court seemed to also imply),

The United States Supreme Court at the time of United States v. Miller *(1939), the last time the Court ruled on the Second Amendment: (seated, from left) Justices Sutherland, McReynolds, Hughes, Brandeis, and Butler; (standing, from left) Justices Cardozo, Stone, Roberts, and Black.*

then citizens could technically possess rocket launchers and missiles, which would clearly be of more use in defending the country than cheap handguns.

Quilici v. Village of Morton Grove

In most cases since *United States v. Miller*, lower federal courts have followed its guidelines and refused to interpret the Second Amendment as guaranteeing an individual's right to own guns. For example, a strict gun control law was passed in Morton Grove, Illinois, in 1981. It banned the ownership of working handguns, except for peace officers, prison officials, members of the armed forces and National Guard, and security guards, as long as owning the gun was part of their official duties. The ordinance exempted licensed gun collectors and owners of antique firearms. Residents who owned handguns could continue to own them, but they were required to keep them at a local gun club instead of at home. The law did not affect long guns such as rifles.

When Victor Quilici and some other residents of Morton Grove challenged this law, a federal appeals court in 1982 stated once again that possession of handguns by individuals is not part of the right to keep and bear arms, but that the right pertains only to militia service. The court ruled that the local law was a reasonable exercise of local police power and that, in any case, the Second Amendment does not apply to the states. The court's decision stated:

> We agree with the district court that the right to keep and bear arms in Illinois is so limited by the police power that a ban on handguns does not violate that right.... [The framers of the Constitution] envisioned that local governments might exercise their police power to restrict, or prohibit, the right to keep and bear handguns.

The Supreme Court declined to hear an appeal of two lower federal court rulings upholding the constitutionality of the law.

Printz v. United States

In 1993, Congress passed the Brady Handgun Violence Prevention Act, which required a five-day waiting period to purchase a handgun and obligated the chief local law enforcement officials, such as county sheriffs, to conduct background checks on people who wanted to buy guns. Two sheriffs, Jay Printz of Ravalli County, Montana, and Richard Mack of Graham County, Arizona, challenged the Brady Bill, arguing that the federal law had placed an undue burden on local law enforcement officials.

In 1997, a bitterly divided U.S. Supreme Court agreed with Printz by a five to four margin. Writing for the majority, Justice Antonin Scalia's opinion insisted that the federal principle of dividing power between the states and the nation was a crucial part of the way that the Constitution protected American liberties. As a result, the federal government could not order state officials to administer federal law under any circumstances. In a concurring (agreeing) opinion, Justice Clarence Thomas concluded that given the Second Amendment's reference to the right of the people to keep and bear arms, Congress probably had no authority to regulate gun sales within a single state under any circumstances. The majority decision was one of the strongest statements by the Supreme Court of state authority since the Civil War. *Printz v. United States* marked the movement of the Supreme Court under Chief Justice William Rehnquist to give more power to the states. It therefore implied that the Second Amendment would not be incorporated through the Fourteenth Amendment to the states any time in the near future.

The four dissenters who disagreed with the decision, led by Justice John Paul Stevens, argued the opposite position: When Congress acted within its power to regulate commerce, a power given specifically by the Constitution, it was supreme and had to be obeyed. Although the Supreme Court's decision relieved local law enforcement officials from performing background checks, they were replaced by a federal record-checking system run by gun dealers in 1989.

United States v. Emerson

In 1998, Dr. Timothy Joe Emerson was under a domestic violence restraining order that forbade him from approaching his estranged wife or her young daughter. He was therefore prohibited by the 1994 Federal Domestic Violence Act from owning a gun. Emerson was arrested after an incident in which he allegedly threatened his wife with a Beretta pistol and pointed it at her. Judge Samuel Cummings, of the U.S. District Court for the Northern District, dismissed the charge and ruled that federal law denying guns to citizens under restraining orders is an unconstitutional violation of the Second Amendment.

In October 2001, the Fifth U.S. Circuit Court of Appeals in New Orleans reversed the trial court's ruling and sent the case back for trial. However, two judges on the three-judge panel declared that they agreed with the individualist interpretation of the Second Amendment. Judge William Garwood stated,

> We reject the collective rights and sophisticated collective rights models for interpreting the Second Amendment. We hold, constant with *Miller*, that it protects the right of individuals, including those not then actually a member of any militia or engaged in active military service or training, to privately possess and bear their own firearms.... We are mindful that almost all our sister circuits have rejected any individual rights view of the Second Amendment. However...all these opinions seem to have done so either on the erroneous assumption that Miller resolved that issue or without sufficient articulated examination of the history and text of the Second Amendment.

The Fifth U.S. Circuit Court of Appeals found that *Miller* supported neither the individual rights nor the collective rights model of the Second Amendment. Instead, the Court claimed that the *Miller* case was about types of weapons (for example, machine guns) and whether or not they were restricted by the Firearms Act of 1934. Although the Fifth U.S. Circuit Court ruled that "the Second Amendment does protect individual rights," it agreed that gun regulations would be legal if they were "limited, narrowly tailored specific exceptions." In essence, the court ruled that although the Second Amendment protected the rights of individuals to own guns, federal gun control laws dealing with specific situations did not violate the Constitution.

President George W. Bush's administration also supported this individualist position. In a letter to the U.S. Supreme Court regarding Emerson's appeal, U.S. solicitor general Theodore Olson wrote, "The current position of the United States is that the Second Amendment more broadly protects the rights of individuals, including persons who are not members of any militia or engaged in active military service or training, to possess and bear their own firearms." However, that right, continued Olson, is "subject to reasonable restrictions designed to prevent possession by unfit persons or to restrict the possession of types of firearms that are particularly suited to criminal misuse."

The issue remains uncertain because in June 2002, the U.S. Supreme Court declined, without comment, to consider the *Emerson* case. Although other federal courts have failed to follow the interpretation of the Fifth Circuit Court in *Emerson,* the refusal of the U.S. Supreme Court to make a definitive statement has led to many challenges to American gun laws on Second Amendment grounds. In the twenty-first century, after more than 200 years, the interpretation of the Second Amendment of the Constitution remains controversial.

Where Do We Go from Here?

Gun ownership in the United States is legal and recognized by law. The U.S. Supreme Court noted in 1994 in the case of *Staples v. United States* that "there is a long tradition of widespread lawful gun ownership by private individuals in this country." Both common law and legislative enactments preserve the right of armed self-defense. Although the U.S. Supreme Court has never specifically incorporated the Second Amendment into the Fourteenth Amendment's guarantees of liberty, it has applied most of the Bill of Rights to the states, and there's no reason to assume that the Second Amendment should be an exception.

On the other hand, the U.S. Supreme Court has never stated that private gun ownership is protected by the Second Amendment. American courts have consistently been reluctant to strike down local, state, and federal gun control laws on the basis of the Second Amendment. No U.S. Supreme Court case has ever supported any Second Amendment-based individual right of Americans to own guns for their own purposes. In only two cases in the entire twentieth century has a federal court declared a gun law to be unconstitutional as a violation of the Second Amendment. The first case was the lower court decision in *United States v. Miller*, which was overturned by the U.S. Supreme Court. The second was the lower court decision in *United States v. Emerson*. If that case is any indication, the American courts will continue to be a battlefield over the interpretation of the Second Amendment well into the twenty-first century.

Glossary

advocacy group—an organization that seeks to persuade people to support a particular viewpoint on a public issue, such as for or against increased restrictions on gun use

amendment—a change or addition to a legal document, such as an amendment to the U.S. Constitution

armory—a place where arms are manufactured

assassination—the premeditated killing of a person, usually a public figure

assault weapons—antipersonnel rifles, shotguns, and handguns designed mainly for military and law enforcement purposes

automatic weapon—a weapon that fires more than one round with a single pull of the trigger

collective right—a right held by the people as a group, not on an individual basis

common law—a system of justice begun in England and spread by the British to the places that they colonized; based on previous court decisions rather than on specific laws

conscientious objector—a person who resists military service for religious reasons or reasons of personal morality

conscription—a government's policy of requiring people to serve in the armed forces

crime rate—the amount of crime, presented in statistical terms

frontier—the part of a country that forms the furthest limits of its settled or inhabited regions

general militia—a militia made up of the entire body of eligible males—the "people" as a whole—that were supposed to participate in a minimum required service

gun control—restrictions on the use and ownership of guns

homicide—murder

inalienable right—a fundamental right that cannot be taken away

incorporation—in constitutional theory, the application to state power of a limit on federal government power

individual right—a right held by the people as individuals

judicial review—the right of the judicial branch of government to interpret the constitutionality of laws

militia—a military organization made up of people who are not professional soldiers

police power—the power of a government to preserve public order and maintain minimum standards of health, safety, and welfare for its citizens

select militia—a militia made up of volunteer units that organize and train frequently, often with their own equipment, uniforms, and unit loyalty

self-defense—an action by an individual to protect himself or herself

standing army—an army that remains in existence at all times, not just during wartime

Bibliography

Books

Akhil, Amar. *The Bill of Rights: Creation and Reconstruction.* New Haven, CT: Yale University Press, 1998.

Bogus, Carl, ed. *The Second Amendment in Law and History.* New York: New Press, 2000.

Cater, Gregg. *The Gun Control Movement.* New York: Twayne, 1997.

Cornell, Saul. *Whose Right to Bear Arms Did the Second Amendment Protect?* Boston: Bedford/St. Martin's, 2000.

Dizard, Jan, et al. *Guns in America: A Reader.* New York: New York University Press, 1999.

Kates, Don, and Gary Kleck. *The Great American Gun Debate.* San Francisco: Pacific Research Institute for Public Policy, 1997.

Kruschke, Earl. *Gun Control: A Reference Handbook.* Santa Barbara, CA: ABC-CLIO, 1995.

Lott, John. *More Guns, Less Crime.* Chicago: University of Chicago Press, 1998.

Spitzer, Robert. *The Right to Bear Arms: Rights and Liberties Under the Law.* Santa Barbara, CA: ABC-CLIO, 2001.

Web Sites

The Brady Campaign to Prevent Gun Violence United with the Million Mom March *www.handguncontrol.org*

The Journalist's Guide to Gun Policy Scholars and Second Amendment Scholars *www.gunscholar.com*

National Rifle Association (NRA) *www.nra.org*

Sources on the Second Amendment and Rights to Keep and Bear Arms in State Constitutions *www1.law.ucla.edu/~volokh/2amteach/sources.htm*

Index

Note: Page numbers in *italics* indicate illustrations and captions.

A
AAP (American Academy of Pediatrics), Vol. 3: 89
Abbott, Stephen, Vol. 3: *12*, 12
Abraham, Nathaniel, Vol. 3: 2
accidental shooting deaths, Vol. 3: 42–43
Act 291, Vol. 2: 115
Adams, Samuel, Vol. 1: 25, *26*
administrative searches, Vol. 3: 65
adolescents, Vol. 3: viii–ix, 2–3, 13–14, 105–106, 108–116, *115*. *See also* youth violence
advertisements, Vol. 3: 110
advocacy group
Vol. 1: 120
Vol. 2: 124
Vol. 3: 123
Vol. 4: 123
African-Americans
Vol. 1: 50–52, 66–67, 98, 110–112, *111*
Vol. 3: 38
Alameda County (CA), Vol. 4: 58
Alaska, Vol. 3: 52
Aleksich, Brock, Vol. 3: 94
Allin Conversion, Vol. 2: 54–55
Allin, Erskine, Vol. 2: 26, 54–55
Amateur Trapshooting Association, Vol. 2: 12
amendment. *See also* Bill of Rights
Vol. 1: vii, 120
Vol. 3: 123
Vol. 4: 123
America, Vol. 1: 8–13, *9*, *12*
American Academy of Pediatrics (AAP), Vol. 3: 89
American Civil War
Vol. 1: 46
Vol. 2: 47–50, *49*
American frontier, Vol. 1: 49–50
American Revolution
Vol. 1: 19–20
Vol. 2: 39
American system of manufacturing, Vol. 2: 34
ammunition
Vol. 1: 75–76
Vol. 3: 75
antifederalists, Vol. 1: 25–26, *26*, 30–32
anti-gun-control advocacy organizations, Vol. 1: 71–72
anti-gun-control measures, Vol. 4: 29–32
Archives of Pediatrics and Adolescent Medicine, Vol. 3: 85
Arkansas, Vol. 3: 52
Arming America (Bellesiles), Vol. 4: 109–110
armory
Vol. 2: 17–19, 23–26, *25*, 29–33, 124
Vol. 4: 123
arms. *See* firearms; right to bear arms
arsenal, Vol. 2: 124
Article VI, U.S. Constitution, Vol. 4: 44
Article VII, British Bill of Rights, Vol. 1: 6–8
Articles of Confederation, Vol. 1: 22, 104
Ashcroft, John
Vol. 1: 100
Vol. 3: 85
Vol. 4: 27, 30–31
Asking Saves Kids (ASK) Campaign, Vol. 3: 88, 89–91
assassination
Vol. 1: 120
Vol. 2: 124
assault weapons
Vol. 1: 81–82, 120
Vol. 2: 7, 124
Vol. 3: 51, 123
Vol. 4: 13, 15, 28, 32, 67, 123
automatic weapon, Vol. 2: 124
Auto-Ordnance, Vol. 2: 68–69, 71
Aymette v. State, Vol. 1: 107–108

B
background checks
Vol. 1: 78–79, 80
Vol. 4: 12, 13, 15, 27, 28, 34, *34*, 35, 41, 55, 56, 60–63
Bailey, Chuck, Vol. 4: 57, *57*
Baird, Laura, Vol. 4: 4, *4*
Baker, Bob, Vol. 4: *53*, 53
ballistic fingerprinting, Vol. 2: *94*, 94–97, *97*
Barber, Gus, Vol. 3: 94–95
BAR (Browning automatic rifle), Vol. 2: 77–78
Barnitz, Frank, Vol. 4: 102
Barr, Bob, Vol. 4: 28
barrel-and-chamber insert, Vol. 3: 78
Barron v. Baltimore, Vol. 1: 30, 107
Barrow, Clyde
Vol. 2: *70*
Vol. 3: 106, *106*
The Basketball Diaries (film), Vol. 3: 114
Bassham, Lanny, Vol. 4: 16
Bath (MI), Vol. 3: 68
Baxter, Andrew, Vol. 3: 92
Beecher, Henry Ward, Vol. 2: 46
Beecher's Bibles, Vol. 2: 45–46
Bell Campaign, Vol. 3: 72
Bellesiles, Michael, Vol. 4: 109–110
Beretta, Vol. 2: 87
Bethel (AK), Vol. 3: 52
Bill of Rights
Vol. 1: 28–32, *33*, 108–110
Vol. 3: 2
Vol. 4: 45–46
Bills of Rights, state
Vol. 1: 32–34
Vol. 4: *49*, 49–51, *50*
The Birth of a Nation (film), Vol. 1: *56*, 56–57
Bjergo, Gary, Vol. 4: 82, *82*
Blacksmith, Hank, Vol. 3: 92
Blanchard, Thomas, Vol. 2: 26, 27–28, 29
Bliss v. Commonwealth, Vol. 1: 107
Bonnie and Clyde (film), Vol. 3: 107
Booth, John Wilkes, Vol. 2: *56*, 56
Borchardt, Hugo, Vol. 2: 81
Boston Massacre, Vol. 1: 13, *15*
boys, Vol. 3: 13–16, 37, 38, 49, 53, 108, 116
Brady Campaign to Prevent Gun Violence, Vol. 1: 78
Brady Handgun Violence Protection Act of 1993
Vol. 1: 79–81, *80*, 102, 116–117
Vol. 2: 14
Vol. 3: 24, 51
Vol. 4: 24, *60*, 60–61
Brady, James
Vol. 1: *77*, 77–78, *80*
Vol. 4: 60, *60*
Brady, Josh, Vol. 3: *15*, 15
Brady, Sarah, Vol. 1: 77–78
Branch Davidians, Vol. 1: 91, *92*
Brandeis, Louis, Vol. 4: 69, *70*
breechloaders, Vol. 2: 50–55, *53*, 61
breech-loading revolver, Vol. 2: 30–31, 44–45
breech-loading rifle, Vol. 2: 23–24, 45–46
Breyer, Stephen, Vol. 3: 59
British army, Vol. 1: *12*, 12–13, *15*
British Bill of Rights, Vol. 1: 6–8
Bronson, Charles, Vol. 4: *75*, 75, 77
Browning automatic rifle (BAR), Vol. 2: 77–78
Browning Duck Hunter (video game), Vol. 3: 112
Browning, John Moses, Vol. 2: 77–78, 81
Brown, John, Vol. 2: 46
bullets
Vol. 1: 75–76
Vol. 2: *viii*, 3, 41–42, 94–97, *97*
Bureau of Alcohol, Tobacco, and Firearms (BATF)
Vol. 1: 74, 89–91, *90*, 93–94
Vol. 2: 95
Vol. 4: 52–53, 54, 55
Burns, Michael, Vol. 1: *73*
Burton, James, Vol. 2: 42
Bush, George H.W.
Vol. 1: 81
Vol. 3: 51
Vol. 4: 32
Bush, George W.
Vol. 1: 118
Vol. 2: 121
Vol. 3: 82
Vol. 4: 12, 24, 25–26, 27, 29, 96–97
Bush, Jeb, Vol. 2: 111, *111*
Butch Cassidy (George Parker), Vol. 3: *105*, 105

C
cable-style safety lock, Vol. 3: *77*, *78*
caliber
Vol. 2: 3, 124
Vol. 3: 123
Vol. 4: 123
California
Vol. 2: 100–101, 102
Vol. 3: 10, 17, 24, 43, 50, 51, 56, *57*, 57, 62, 66, 79, 80
Vol. 4: 40–41, *47*, 47–48, 55, 58, 63, 66–69, *68*, 71, *71*, 100
California Rifle & Pistol Association v. City of West Hollywood, Vol. 4: 47–48
Calling Forth Act of 1792, Vol. 1: 41–42
Canada, Vol. 3: 56
cannons, Vol. 2: 4, *50*
CAP laws. *See* child access prevention (CAP) laws
Capone, Al, Vol. 1: 57–58, *59*
Carnahan, Jean, Vol. 4: 27
cartoons, violent, Vol. 3: 108, 116
cartridge
Vol. 2: 3, 42, 124
Vol. 3: 123
Caskey, Harold, Vol. 4: 101, *101*
Catholics, Vol. 1: 5–6
Cato's Letters (Trenchard and Gordon), Vol. 1: 10
Catt, Carrie Chapman, Vol. 4: x
CCW. *See* concealed weapons, carrying
CDA (Communications Decency Act), Vol. 3: 121
censorship, Vol. 3: 117–118, 120–121
Centers for Disease Control (CDC)
Vol. 3: viii, 32
Vol. 4: 114–117
Cermak, Anton
Vol. 1: 61
Vol. 2: 71
Chang, Henry, Vol. 4: *47*, 47
Charles II, King of England, Vol. 1: 5
Cheney, Dick, Vol. 4: 25
child access prevention (CAP) laws, Vol. 3: 16–19, *17*, *18*, 43
children. *See also* schools; youth violence
Vol. 3:
access to guns, 10–12, *11*
child access prevention laws, 16–19
curiosity about guns, 12–14
deaths/injuries from guns, viii–ix
guns in movies/television, 108–110
hunting and, 4–10, *5*, *6*, *9*
juvenile gun court, 19–20
laws for protection of, 2–4
parents ideas about guns and, 14–15
self-defense by children, 31–32

suicide and, *34*, 34–42, *37*, *39*
symbolic power of guns for, 15–16
violence in mass media, 113–116, *115*
violence in television, 105–106
violence in video games, 110–113
children, protection of
Vol. 3:
Child Safety Lock Act, 83–85, *84*
child safety/self-defense, 79–80
Eddie Eagle program, 86–88, *87*
firearms education, 85–86
gun control legislation, *83*
gun locks, *77*, 77–79, *78*
gun safes, 76–77
gun safety lawsuits, *95*, 95–98
guns at neighbor's house, 88–91, *90*
need for, 72
Project HomeSafe, *81*, 81–83
Remington Model 700, 92–95, *93*
smart guns, *89*, *96*, 98–102, *99*, *100*
unsafe firearms storage, *73*, 73–76, *74*
unsafe guns, 91–92
Child Safety Lock Act, Vol. 3: 83–85, *84*
Chippokes Plantation State Park (VA), Vol. 3: 6, *6*
Chivington, John, Vol. 1: 50
"the Cincinnati Revolt," Vol. 4: 39
Cincinnatus complex, Vol. 1: 15–16
Citizen's Committee for the Right to Keep and Bear Arms, Vol. 1: 72
City Year volunteer group, Vol. 3: 26, *26*
civil rights movement, Vol. 4: 38
Clemens, Samuel, Vol. 2: 31–32
Cleveland Elementary School (Stockton, CA), Vol. 3: 51
Clinton, Bill
Vol. 1: 79–80, *80*
Vol. 3: 62, *119*
Vol. 4: 8, 24, 26, *26*, 60, *60*
Coalition to Stop Gun Violence (CSGV), Vol. 1: 78
Cobourg (Germany), Vol. 4: 10, *10*
Cole, Jeff, Vol. 3: 112, *112*
Colfax Massacre, Vol. 1: 110–112, *111*
collective right, Vol. 1: 84–86, *85*, 120
collectors, Vol. 2: 13–14
Collins, Diane, Vol. 3: 12
Colorado
Vol. 3: 8, 26, *33*, 41, *41*, 42, *42*, 53–55, *54*, 60–62
Vol. 4: 27, 41, 48, 56, *65*, 65–66, *66*
Colt, Vol. 2: 72–74, 78, 79, 80, 84
Colt Armory, Vol. 2: 30–33
Colt Manufacturing Company, Vol. 3: 89, *89*, *96*, 96
Colt, Samuel, Vol. 2: 30–33, *31*, 44–45
Columbine High School (Littleton, CO)
Vol. 1: vii, 102
Vol. 2: 14
Vol. 3: 53–55, 60–62
Vol. 4: 8–11, *9*, 23–24, 28
commerce clause
Vol. 3: 123
Vol. 4: 123
Committee on the Machinery of the United States, Vol. 2: 33–34
Committee to Study Youth Violence, Vol. 3: 69–70
common law, Vol. 1: 2–3, 104–105, *105*, 120
Commonwealth v. Alger, Vol. 1: 106
Communications Decency Act (CDA), Vol. 3: 121
concealed-carry permit, Vol. 4: 98–102
concealed weapons, carrying (CCW)
Vol. 4:
ban on carrying, 13, 15, 28
controversy of, 97–98
handguns, *104*
handgun training session, *103*
history of, 96–97
John Lott's survey, 109–111
laws, 102–105
march about, *97*, 97
in Missouri, 100–102, *101*
pro-concealed gun rally, *98*, 98
Richard Rhee with AK-47, *110*
self-defense and, 106–109, *107*, *108*
"shall-issue"/"may issue" states, 98–100
state laws, 111–112
Concepcion, Mike, Vol. 3: *25*
Congress. *See* U.S. Congress
Congress of Racial Equality (CORE), Vol. 1: 98
Connecticut, Vol. 3: 17
conscientious objector, Vol. 1: 120
conscription, Vol. 1: 3–4, 120
Constitution. *See* U.S. Constitution
Constitutional Convention, Vol. 1: x
Consumer Product Safety Commission (CPSC)
Vol. 2: 106–109, *108*
Vol. 3: 83
consumer safety standards, Vol. 2: 106–109, *108*
Conyers (GA), Vol. 3: 61–62, 67–68
Coonfare, Jesse, Vol. 3: 92
Corbett, Ellen, Vol. 4: 68, *68*
CORE (Congress of Racial Equality), Vol. 1: 98
Cotto, Efrain, Vol. 4: *33*, 33
Cox, Chris, Vol. 2: 123
Craig, H., Vol. 2: 42
Craig, Larry
Vol. 2: 121
Vol. 4: 35
crime
Vol. 1: 96–98
Vol. 2: 10, 90
Vol. 4: *78*
Bernhard Goetz, 77–79, *78*
CCW laws and, 102–103
crime rates, 74–75
gun control legislation and, 11–12
guns and self-defense, 81–83, *82*, *86*
justifiable homicide, 79–81
movies about, *75*, 75–77
National Crime Victimization Surveys, 83–87, *85*
in twenty-first century, 92–94, *93*
weapon use/violent crime from 1993 to 2001, 88–90
women/justifiable homicide, *90*, 90–92
Crime in the United States (Federal Bureau of Investigation), Vol. 4: 92–93
crime rate
Vol. 1: 120
Vol. 2: 124
Vol. 3: 22, *23*, 23–24, 26–27, 46, 123
Vol. 4: 123
Cromwell, Oliver, Vol. 1: 5
Crystal Palace Exposition, Vol. 2: 45
CSGV (Coalition to Stop Gun Violence), Vol. 1: 78
Cummings, Homer, Vol. 1: 60–61
Cummings, Samuel, Vol. 1: 117
cycle of outrage, Vol. 1: 101–102

D

Daily Telegraph, Vol. 2: 61–62
Daisy Manufacturing, Vol. 2: 109
Daley, Richard M., Vol. 4: 49
Dartmouth, Lord, Vol. 1: 14
Daschle, Tom, Vol. 4: 32
Davis, Gray, Vol. 4: 71, *71*
Davis Industries, Vol. 2: 117
Davis, Jefferson, Vol. 2: 41, 43, 50
Dean, Howard, Vol. 4: 33
deaths, Vol. 3: viii–ix, 16, 42–43, 49, 55. *See also* homicide; suicide
Death Wish (film), Vol. 4: 75, *75*, *77*
Declaration of Independence, Vol. 1: 17, 18–19
Dees-Thomases, Donna, Vol. 4: *14*, 14
defective guns, Vol. 3: 91–98, *93*, *95*
defensive gun use, estimates of, Vol. 4: vii
Degan, William, Vol. 1: 90
Delaware, Vol. 3: 18
DeLay, Tom, Vol. 4: 29
Deming Middle School (NM), Vol. 3: 62
democracy, Vol. 4: 2
Democratic Party
Vol. 1: 72–73
Vol. 4: 20–29, *26*, 32–33, 35, 42
DeNiro, Robert, Vol. 3: 109, *109*
Denver (CO)
Vol. 3: 26, *33*, 41, *41*
Vol. 4: 48
depression, Vol. 3: 34
Derringer, Henry, Vol. 2: *56*, 56
Derringers, Vol. 2: *56*, 56
Diamond Street gang, Vol. 3: 48, *48*
DiCaprio, Leonardo, Vol. 3: 114
Dingell, John
Vol. 1: 94
Vol. 4: 32, 35
division of labor, Vol. 2: 124
Dolan, Peg, Vol. 3: *83*, 83
Donohue, John, Vol. 4: 107
Doom (video game), Vol. 3: 112–113
draftee, Vol. 1: 4
Dred Scott case, Vol. 1: 50–51
drinking age, Vol. 4: 70
Dukes, Tawana, Vol. 3: 64–65
Dunblane Primary School (Scotland), Vol. 3: 56
Durbin, Richard, Vol. 2: 121
Dyer, Alexander, Vol. 2: 53–54

E

Eddie Eagle Program, Vol. 3: 86–88, *87*
Edinboro (PA), Vol. 3: 52, 56, 80
Edwards, Larry, Vol. 3: *81*
Edwards, Stephen, Vol. 3: 91
Eisenhower, Dwight, Vol. 2: *76*, 76–77
Emerson, Timothy Joe, Vol. 1: 117–118
Emerson v. United States
Vol. 1: xiv, 117–118
Vol. 4: 31
England, Vol. 1: 2–6, *4*
English Civil War, Vol. 1: *4*, 5–6
entertainment industry, Vol. 3: x. *See also* mass media
Entertainment Software Rating Boards, Vol. 3: 111
exports, Vol. 2: 60–62, 72–74

F

Fabrique Nationale (FN), Vol. 2: 77–78, 92
Fair Park High School (LA), Vol. 4: *vii*, vii
Fayetteville (TN), Vol. 3: 52
Federal Aviation Act of 1958, Vol. 1: 64
Federal Bureau of Investigation, Vol. 4: 92–93
Federal Firearms Act of 1938, Vol. 1: 62, 64
federal handgun registration, Vol. 4: 7
The Federalist Papers (Hamilton, Madison, and Jay), Vol. 1: 27
federalists, Vol. 1: 25–26
federal system and guns
Vol. 4:
California, 66–69, *68*, *71*
firearms in state Bills of Rights, *49*, 49–51, *50*
"gun show loophole," *53*, 53–56, *54*
gun shows on publicly owned property, 56–58, *57*
laboratory of the states, 69–72
Millsap family, *44*, 44
national government powers, 44
preemption, 46–48, *47*

private gun sales, 51–53
referendums, 63–66, *65*, *66*
registration of guns, 58–59
state powers, 44–46
United States v. Lopez, 48–49
waiting periods, *60*, 60–63, *62*
Feighan, Edward, Vol. 1: 79
Fifth U.S. Circuit Court, Vol. 1: 117–118
Finland, Vol. 3: 33
firearm
Vol. 2: 124
Vol. 3: 123
Vol. 4: 123
Firearm Owners Protection Act of 1986, Vol. 1: 73, 74–75
firearms. *See also* guns; storage of firearms
Vol. 1: 5–6, 49–50, 57–60, *59*
Vol. 2: *vii*, vii–x, 2–14, *5*, *6*, *11*
Vol. 3: viii–x, 15–16, 35–36, 85–88, *87*
Vol. 4: *49*, 49–51, *50*
firearms industry. *See also* manufacturer's product liability
Vol. 2: vii–x, *vii*, *viii*, 21–23, 90–91, 99–100, 104, 110–111, *120*, 120–123, *123*
Vol. 3: 8–10, 95–98
Vol. 4: 31–32
firearms industry, 19th century
Vol. 2:
Beecher's Bibles, 45–46
breechloaders, 50–52
bullets, changes in, 41–42
final developments in, 57–58
handguns, competition in, 55–56, *56*
Harpers Ferry arsenal, 46–47
"Kentucky rifle," 36–38
military tactics, 38–40, *40*
percussion cap, 40–41
Remington and Winchester, 57
repeating rifles, 52–54
rifle-musket, 42–44, *43*
rifle-musket and Civil War, *47*, 47–50
Samuel Colt's revolver, 44–45
Springfield Armory/Allin Conversion, 54–55
firearms industry, rise of mass production
Vol. 2:
American system of manufacturing, 34
armory need and, 17–19
Colt Armory, 30–33
Committee on the Machinery of the United States, 33–34
federal government and, 17
Harpers Ferry armory, 23–24
mass production of firearms, 16–17
patent arms, 29–30
Simeon North and, 19–21, *21*
Springfield Armory firearms production, 24–26, *25*
U.S. Army Ordnance Department and, 26–27
use of gauges/lathe, 27–29, *28*
firearms industry, 20th century
Vol. 2:
American, in 2000, 86–87
Bill Ruger, 85–86, *86*
Browning automatic rifle, 77–78
changes in gun industry, 83–85
exports, 60–62, *61*
future of, 87–88
Garand M-1 semiautomatic rifle, 74–75, *75*
Gatling gun, *64*, 64–65
gun control, rise of, 82–83
Krag rifle, 62–63, *63*
M-16 rifle, 78–80, *79*
machine gun and World War I, 67–68
machine gun improvements, 65–67, *66*
machine guns in 1930s, *70*, 70–71
military-industrial complex and, *76*, 76–77
Nye Committee, 72–74, *73*
regulation, 71–72
semiautomatic pistols, rise of, 80–82, *81*, *82*
tommy gun, 68–70, *69*
U.S. Rifle Model 1903, 63–64
Firearms Owners' Protection Act, Vol. 4: 23, 52
firearms-related death, Vol. 3: 32–33
First Amendment
Vol. 3: 117, 118
Vol. 4: 57
flintlock, Vol. 2: 4, 36, 40
Florida
Vol. 3: 17, 19, 65
Vol. 4: 52, 55, 64, 99
Florida Game and Fresh Water Fish Commission, Vol. 3: 10
FN (Fabrique Nationale), Vol. 2: 77–78, 92
Ford, Vol. 2: 106
Forsyth, Alexander, Vol. 2: 40
Fortas, Abe, Vol. 3: 63
Fort Gibson Middle School (OK), Vol. 3: 62
Fortifications Appropriations Act of 1888, Vol. 2: 62
Foster, Carolyn, Vol. 3: 12
Fourteenth Amendment
Vol. 1: 30, 108–112, *109*
Vol. 4: 45
Freedmen's Bureau Act of 1866, Vol. 1: 52
French and Indian War, Vol. 2: 39
frontier, Vol. 1: 120
Fucile, Joe, Vol. 4: *103*, 103
fully automatic guns. *See* machine guns

G
Gage, Thomas, Vol. 1: 14–15
Gallup poll, Vol. 4: 2–3, *3*
gangs, Vol. 3: 24–26, *25*, 47–48, *48*, *115*
gangsters
Vol. 1: 57–60, *59*
Vol. 2: 69–70
Garand, John, Vol. 2: 26, 74–75, *75*
Garand M-1 semiautomatic rifle, Vol. 2: 74–75, *75*
Garris, Jordan, Vol. 3: 97
Garwood, William, Vol. 1: 117
Gatling gun, Vol. 2: *64*, 64–65, 66
Gatling, Richard, Vol. 2: 65
gauges, Vol. 2: 27
Gaynor, William, Vol. 1: 57
gender, Vol. 4: 9, 14–16
general militia, Vol. 1: 120
geography, Vol. 4: *33*, 33–35
Georgia, Vol. 3: 61–62, 67–68
Gerbner's Cultural Indicators, Vol. 3: 113
Gerry, Elbridge, Vol. 1: 35
girls, Vol. 3: 38
Giuliani, Rudolph, Vol. 4: 32
Glasser, Harold, Vol. 1: 68
Glendening, Parris, Vol. 2: 101
GOA. *See* Gun Owners of America
The Godfather: Part II (film), Vol. 3: 109, *109*
Goetz, Bernhard, Vol. 4: 77–79, *78*
Gordon, Thomas, Vol. 1: 10
Gore, Al, Vol. 4: 23–24, 26–27
Great Britain, Vol. 1: *4*, 5–6, 11–16, *12*, *15*, *16*
Great Western Gun Show, Vol. 3: *11*, 11
Grover Cleveland Elementary School (San Diego, CA), Vol. 3: 50
Grunow, Barry, Vol. 3: 68–69, *69*
Grunow, Pamela, Vol. 3: *69*, 69
Grunow v. Valor Corporation of Florida, Vol. 3: 68–69, *69*
gun accidents
Vol. 2: 90, 98, 99–100
Vol. 3: 75–76
gun advocates, Vol. 4: x, *85*, 85–87
gun control
Vol. 1: viii, 98, 100, 101–102, 120
Vol. 2: 71–72, 82–83, 85–86, 124
Vol. 3: *viii*, *33*, 72, 123
Vol. 4: 23–26, 32–42, *33*, *37*, *38*, 114–117, 123
Gun Control Act of 1968
Vol. 1: 62, 67–68, 74
Vol. 4: 21, 51–52
gun control legislation. *See also* federal system and guns
Vol. 1:
anti-gun-control advocacy organizations, 71–72
Assault Weapons Ban of 1994, 81–82
Brady campaign to prevent gun violence, 76–78, *77*
Brady Handgun Violence Protection Act of 1993, 79–81, *80*
cop-killer bullets, 75–76
Firearm Owners Protection Act of 1986, 74–75
Gun Control Act of 1968, 67–68, 74
hot summers and, *66*, 66–67
in 1920s, 58
National Firearms Act of 1934, 61–62
National Rifle Association and, 69–71, *70*
political assassinations and, 64–66, *65*
political parties and, 72–73, *73*
Second Amendment and, 82
waiting periods, 78–79
Vol. 4: 15, 16–18, 20–23, 28–29
gun control measures, Vol. 4: *6*, 6–8, 11–12
gun control movement, Vol. 1: 102
gun control regulations, Vol. 4: 46–48, *47*
gun control sponsors, Vol. 4: x
gun dealers, Vol. 3: 4
gun distribution lawsuits, Vol. 2: *111*, 111–114, *113*
Gun-Free School Zones Act
Vol. 3: 56–57, 59–60
Vol. 4: 48–49
gun industry. *See* firearms industry
gun locks, Vol. 3: *73*, 73–85, *77*, *78*, *81*, *84*
gun ownership
Vol. 1: 84–87, *85*
Vol. 4: vii, 7, 34–35
Gun Owners of America (GOA)
Vol. 1: 72
Vol. 2: 100
Vol. 3: 60, 80
gunpowder, Vol. 2: 3–5
gun purchase permits, Vol. 4: 7
gun regulation, Vol. 4: 45–46, 117–122, *119*, *120*
guns. *See also* federal system and guns; firearms; mass media; polls and guns
Vol. 1:
American militia and, 40
antebellum state courts and, 107–108
change in federal policy towards, 60–61
colonial America and, 8, *9*
court cases, 110–119
English Civil War and, 5–6
firearms in frontier, 49–50
gangsters and, 57–60, *59*
in American culture, xi–xii
militia in America and, 11
National Firearms Act of 1934, 61–62
police and, 54–55
popular fiction and, 55–57, *56*
Second Amendment debate, xii–xiii
urban social disorder and, 52–53
Vol. 2: vii–x, *vii*, 3, 42–43
Vol. 3:
child access prevention laws, 16–19, *17*
children and hunting, 4–8, *5*, *6*
children's curiosity about, 12–14
children's easy access to, 10–12, *11*
children's legal use of, *vii*, vii
deaths/injuries from, viii–ix
gangs and, 24–26, *25*
homicides by children and, *30*, 30
in movies/television, 108–110, *109*
juvenile gun court, 19–20

law restricts children and guns, 3–4
mass media violence, 113–116
parents' ideas about, 14–15
protection of children from, ix–x
recruiting children to hunt, 8–10, *9*
suicide and, *34*, 34–42, *37*, *39*
symbolic power of, for children, 15–16
teenagers carrying guns, 27–29, *29*
video games and, 110–113
young people as victims of homicide and, 31
youth violence and, 22–24, *23*, *26*, 26–27
Vol. 4:
crime rates and, 74–75
debate over, 114–117, *115*, *116*, 121–122
emotional issue of, ix–x
gun regulation as symbolic issue, 117–121, *119*, *120*
in twenty-first century, 92–94, *93*
justifiable homicide and, 81
number of/uses for, vii
public opinion and, vii–ix
self-defense and, 81–83, *82*, 86–87
women/justifiable homicide, 90–92
Guns & Ammo (magazine), Vol. 3: 9
gun safes, Vol. 3: 76–77
gun safety
Vol. 2:
ballistic fingerprinting, *94*, 94–97, *97*
debate over, 90–91
firearms industry and, 104
gun sale limitations, 101–104, *103*
New Jersey's smart gun law, 93–94
smart guns, *91*, 91–93
trigger locks, 98–101, *99*
Vol. 3:
Child Safety Lock Act, 83–85, *84*
child safety/self-defense, 79–80
Eddie Eagle program, 86–88, *87*
firearms education for children, 85–86
gun control legislation, *83*
gun locks, *77*, 77–79, *78*
gun safes, 76–77
gun safety lawsuits, *95*, 95–98
guns at neighbor's house, 88–91, *90*
lawsuits, 95–98
need for, 72
Project HomeSafe, *81*, 81–83
Remington Model 700, 92–95, *93*
smart guns, *89*, *96*, 98–102, *99*, *100*
unsafe firearms storage, *73*, 73–76, *74*
unsafe guns, 91–92
gun sales
Vol. 2: 101–104, *103*
Vol. 4: 51–58, *53*, *54*, *57*, 79
guns and schools
Vol. 3:
Columbine High School massacre, 53–55, *54*, 60–62
Committee to Study Youth Violence, 69–70
crimes at schools, 46–47
decline of school violence, 55–56
gangs in schools, 47–48, *48*
Grunow v. Valor Corporation of Florida, 68–69, *69*
gun-free school zones, 56–57, *57*
guns and, 49–50
metal detectors in, 62–65, *63*, *64*
rampage school shootings, 46, *47*, 50–53, *51*
random student gun searches, 65–66
safe gun storage at home, 66–68, *67*
school shooting in Red Lion (PA), *61*
United States v. Lopez, *58*, 58–60
gun shows
Vol. 1: 102
Vol. 2: 14
Vol. 4: 11, *53*, 53–58, *54*, *57*
Guns Magazine, Vol. 3: 111–112
gun use, Vol. 1: viii–x, *ix*, 99–101

H
Haas, Robert, Vol. 2: 112
Halliday v. Sturm, Ruger, Vol. 3: 97
Hall, John H., Vol. 2: 23–24, 51
Hamilton, Alexander, Vol. 1: 27
Hamilton, Thomas, Vol. 3: 56
Hammer, Marion, Vol. 3: 9
Handgun Control, Inc. (HCI)
Vol. 1: 77–79
Vol. 4: 39–40
handguns
Vol. 1: ix, 79–81
Vol. 2:
accidental shooting deaths, 42–43
competition in, 55–56, *56*
defined, 2
semiautomatic pistols, rise of, 80–82, *81*, *82*
types of, 9–10
Vol. 3:
laws relative to children and, 4
safe storage of, 75
suicide and, 35–36
teenagers carrying, 27–29
trigger lock on, *18*
youth violence and, *26*, 26–27
Vol. 4: 7, 8, 28, 79, 118
Harpers Ferry Armory, Vol. 2: 23–24, 41
Harpers Ferry arsenal, Vol. 2: 46–47, *47*
Harris, Eric, Vol. 4: *9*, 9
Harris poll, Vol. 4: 7, 8, 10
Harvard Injury Control Research Center, Vol. 3: 40
Hatch, Orrin
Vol. 3: 117, *117*
Vol. 4: 29–30
Hattori, Yoshihiro, Vol. 1: 101
Hawaii, Vol. 3: 17
Hayek, Stan, Vol. 3: *9*
HCI (Handgun Control, Inc.)
Vol. 1: 77–79
Vol. 4: 39–40
Head, John, Vol. 3: *41*, 41
heavy arms, Vol. 2: 2
Henry, Benjamin Tyler, Vol. 2: 57
Henry, Patrick, Vol. 1: 30
Heritage High School (Conyers, GA), Vol. 3: 61–62
Heston, Charlton
Vol. 1: *70*
Vol. 3: 9
Vol. 4: 22, *22*, 37, *37*
Hinckley, John, Jr., Vol. 1: 74
Hobbes, Thomas, Vol. 1: 19
Holden, Bob, Vol. 4: 102
Hollywood. *See also* mass media
Vol. 1: 60
Vol. 3: 107–108
homicide. *See also* justifiable homicide
Vol. 1: 97, 120
Vol. 2: 124
Vol. 3:
by children, 30, *30*
by youth, handguns and, 26–27
Columbine High School massacre, 53–55
deaths from firearms, 114
decrease in, 23–24
defined, 123
from gunshot wounds, viii–ix
guns and schools, 49
mass media and, 104
of children by gun, 72
of women, 91
rampage school shootings, 50–53, *51*
rates for children, 22
rates of, 74
in twenty-first century, 92–93
U.S. rates vs. other countries, 32–33
young people as victims, 31
youth gang homicides, 26
Vol. 4: 89–90
Hood, John Bell, Vol. 2: 50
HR 1036. *See* Protection of Legal Commerce in Arms Act
HR 1056/S, Vol. 2: x
Hughes, Jessie, Vol. 4: *65*, 65
hunting
Vol. 1: 8, *9*, 48–49, 98–99
Vol. 3: 4–10, *5*, *6*, *9*
hunting license, Vol. 3: 8
hunting weapons, Vol. 2: 7–9, *8*

I
IBIS (Integrated Ballistic Identification System), Vol. 2: 95–96
ILA (Institute for Legislative Action), Vol. 1: 71
Illinois
Vol. 3: 4, 17, *17*
Vol. 4: 49, 50, 58, 61–62
Illustrated London News, Vol. 2: 45
inalienable right
Vol. 1: 121
Vol. 4: 123
incorporation, Vol. 1: 108–110, 121
Indiana, Vol. 4: 57
individual right
Vol. 1: 86–87, 117–118, 121
Vol. 4: 123
Injury Prevention Program at Children's Hospital in Boston, Vol. 3: 15
Institute for Legislative Action (ILA), Vol. 1: 71
Integrated Ballistic Identification System (IBIS), Vol. 2: 95–96
Internet gun sales, Vol. 4: 13, 15, *17*, 17, 28
It Can Happen Here (film), Vol. 1: 94

J
James II, King of England, Vol. 1: 5–6, *7*
Jay, John, Vol. 1: 27
Jefferson, Thomas
Vol. 1: 20
Vol. 2: 22–23
Jim Crow laws, Vol. 1: 52
Johann Gutenberg secondary school, Vol. 3: 56
John McDonogh High School (LA), Vol. 3: 64, *64*
Johnson, Lyndon, Vol. 3: 113
Johnston, Joseph, Vol. 2: 50
Jonesboro (AR), Vol. 3: 52
Journal of the American Medical Association, Vol. 3: 106
judicial review, Vol. 1: 121
"junk guns." *See* "Saturday night specials"
justices, Vol. 1: 104
justifiable homicide, Vol. 4: 79–80, 81, 89, *90*, 90–92, 106, 123
juvenile gun court, Vol. 3: 19–20

K
Kansas-Nebraska Act, Vol. 2: 45
Kasler v. Lockyer, Vol. 4: 69
Keep Your Family Safe from Firearm Injury (AAP), Vol. 3: 102
Kehoe, Andrew, Vol. 3: 68
Kennedy, Edward, Vol. 1: 65
Kennedy, Harry, Vol. 4: *101*, 101
Kennedy, John F.
Vol. 1: 64–65
Vol. 4: 6
Kentucky
Vol. 3: *viii*, 52, 114
Vol. 4: 100
"Kentucky rifle," Vol. 2: 38
Kentucky state court, Vol. 1: 107
Kephart, Horace, Vol. 1: 58
Killeen (TX), Vol. 3: 51
King, Martin Luther, Jr., Vol. 1: xii, *xiii*, 65
Kinkade, John, Vol. 4: *34*, 34
Klebold, Dylan, Vol. 4: *9*, 9
Kleck, Gary, Vol. 4: 87, 103–104, 106–107, 111
Knox, Henry, Vol. 2: 17, *18*, 19

Kohl, Herb, Vol. 3: *84*, 84, 85
Koresh, David, Vol. 1: 91, *92*
Krag-Jorgenson rifle, Vol. 2: 62-63, *63*
KTW bullets, Vol. 1: 75-76

L
lathe, Vol. 2: 27-28, *28*
Lathrup, Stephanie, Vol. 3: *5*
law enforcement officers, Vol. 4: 76, 92-93, 96
Law Enforcement Officers Protection Act of 1986, Vol. 1: 76
laws, Vol. 3: 2-4, 16-19, *17*, 56-57, 99-100. *See also* gun control legislation
lawsuits
Vol. 1: 113
Vol. 2: 106, 109-116, *111*, *113*, *114*, 120-123
Vol. 3: 51, *58*, 58-60, 63-65, 68-69, 95-98
Layton, Frank, Vol. 1: 113
Lee, Robert E., Vol. 2: 50
Lee, Roswell, Vol. 2: 26, 27
legal immunity
Vol. 2: *120*, 120-123, *123*, 124
Vol. 4: 123
Lennon, John
Vol. 1: 77
Vol. 4: *6*, 6
Lethal Force Institute, Vol. 3: 56
Levin, Carl, Vol. 2: 117
liability. *See also* manufacturer's product liability
Vol. 2: 124
Vol. 3: 123
Vol. 4: 123
Liddy, G. Gordon, Vol. 1: 94
Lincoln, Abraham, Vol. 4: viii
Littleton (CO), Vol. 3: *42*, 42, 53-55, *54*, 60-62
lobby, Vol. 4: 37
lobbying, Vol. 4: *37*, 37-41, *38*
Locke High School (Los Angeles, CA), Vol. 3: 66
Locke, John, Vol. 1: 18
Lockyer, Bill, Vol. 4: 68, *68*
long guns
Vol. 2: 2
Vol. 3: 4-8, *5*, *6*
Lopez, Alfonso, Jr.
Vol. 3: 58-60
Vol. 4: 48-49
Lorcin Engineering, Vol. 2: *116*, 116-117
Los Angeles (CA)
Vol. 3: 24, 66
Vol. 4: 58
Lott, John, Vol. 4: 106, 108-111
Louisiana, Vol. 3: vii, *vii*
Ludwig, Jens, Vol. 4: 106-107

M
M-16 rifle, Vol. 2: *6*, 7, 78-80, *79*
M1903 rifle, Vol. 2: 63-64
MacArthur, Douglas, Vol. 2: 75
Machiavelli, Niccolò, Vol. 1: 17, *18*
machine guns, Vol. 2: 3, *64*, 64-71, *66*, *69*, *70*, 77-78
Mack, Richard, Vol. 1: 116
Madison, James, Vol. 1: *xi*, 24, 27, 28-29, 33-34, 44, 45, 88, 89
magazine
Vol. 1: 77
Vol. 2: 125
Vol. 3: 123
Vol. 4: 124
Mahoney, John T., Vol. 2: 109
mail-order gun sales, Vol. 4: 13, 15, 28
Malcom X, Vol. 1: 65
Manhattan (NY), Vol. 3: 24
Manson, Marilyn, Vol. 3: 117, *117*
manufacturer's product liability, Vol. 2: 106-123, *107*, *108*, *111*, *113*, *114*, *116*, *118*, *120*, *123*
Martin, Luther, Vol. 1: *31*
Maryland
Vol. 2: 101
Vol. 3: 99
Vol. 4: 63-64
Mason, George, Vol. 1: 30
Massachusetts
Vol. 1: 13, 14-15, 22-23, *23*
Vol. 3: 18-19, *74*, 74
Vol. 4: 63
mass media
Vol. 3:
Bonnie and Clyde, *106*
Butch Casssidy and gang, *105*
complaints about violence in, 106-108
gang initiation and, *115*
guns in, 108-110, *109*
influence on gun popularity, x
lull in issue of, 121-122
Telecommunications Act of 1996, *119*, 120-121
video games, 110-113, *111*
violence and, 104-106
violence in television, *112*
violence, solutions for, 116-119
violent media, effects of, 113-116
matchlocks, Vol. 2: 4
Mathieu, Ross, Vol. 3: 96-97
Maxim, Hiram, Vol. 2: 65-66, *66*, 67
may-issue states, Vol. 4: 100
McCabe, Chad, Vol. 4: *50*, 50
McCarthy, Carolyn, Vol. 4: 26, *26*, 35
McClure, James, Vol. 1: 75
McClure-Volkmer Act, Vol. 4: 52
McGreevey, James
Vol. 2: 93
Vol. 3: *100*, 100
McReynolds, James, Vol. 1: 114
McVeigh, Timothy, Vol. 1: *95*, 95-96
media. *See* mass media
men, Vol. 4: 14-15
Merced (CA), Vol. 3: 80
metal detectors, Vol. 3: *23*, 62-65, *63*
metallic cartridges, Vol. 2: 51-52, 55, 62
Metzenbaum, Howard
Vol. 1: 79
Vol. 2: *108*, 108
Mexican War, Vol. 2: 41, 48
Mfume, Kweisi, Vol. 2: *113*
Michigan, Vol. 4: 59
Michigan Department of State Police v. Sitz, Vol. 3: 65
Mikulski, Barbara, Vol. 2: 122-123, *123*
Military Company of Massachusetts, Vol. 1: 10-11
military-industrial complex, Vol. 2: 76-77
military, U.S., Vol. 2: *6*, 6-7. *See also* U.S. Army
militia
Vol. 1:
in America, *10*, 10-11
in American Revolution, 19-20
Articles of Confederation on, 22
Calling Forth Act and Whiskey Rebellion, 41-42
decline of, 45-47
defined, 121
gun ownership rights and, 84-86, *85*
history of, *3*, 3-5
in Massachusetts, 14-16, *16*
National Guard becomes, 47-48
new militia movement, 92-93, 95-96
Presser v. Illinois and, 112-113
right to revolution and, 88-89
Second Amendment and, 30-32, 34-35
Uniform Militia Act of 1792, 40-41
U.S. Constitution and, 24-25, 27
War of 1812, 42-45, *44*
Vol. 2: 125
Vol. 4: 124
Militia Act of 1903, Vol. 1: 47
Miller, Jack, Vol. 1: 113
Miller, Jim, Vol. 4: *25*, 25
Miller v. Texas, Vol. 1: 113
"Million Mom March"
Vol. 3: 62
Vol. 4: 9, *14*, 14
Millsap family, Vol. 4: 44, *44*, 89, *89*, *120*, 120
Minié, Claude, Vol. 2: 41
Minnesota, Vol. 4: 48, 111, 116, *116*
Mississippi, Vol. 3: *47*, 47, 52, 55-56
Missouri
Vol. 3: 110-111
Vol. 4: 64, 100-102, *101*
Mordecai, Alfred, Vol. 2: 46
More Guns, Less Crime (Lott), Vol. 4: 106
Morgan, Daniel, Vol. 1: *43*
Morial, Marc, Vol. 2: 115
Morris, Gouverneur, Vol. 1: 45
Morton Grove (IL), Vol. 1: 115
Moses Lake (WA), Vol. 3: 52
movies, Vol. 3: 104-110, *109*, 113-119
municipal lawsuits, Vol. 2: *114*, 114-116
munitions, Vol. 2: 125
murder. *See also* homicide
Vol. 1: 57
Vol. 3: 22, 23-24, 106
Vol. 4: vii
Murdock, Margaret, Vol. 4: 16
music videos, Vol. 3: 106
Mustard, David, Vol. 4: 106, 110-111

N
NAACP v. Accu-Tek, Vol. 2: 113-114
Nash, Sylvester, Vol. 2: 28
National Association for the Advancement of Colored People (NAACP), Vol. 2: *113*, 113
National Coalition to Ban Handguns (NCBH), Vol. 1: 78
National Commission on the Causes and Prevention of Violence, Vol. 3: 113
National Crime Victimization Survey (NCVS), Vol. 4: vii, 74, 82-90, *85*
National Defense Act, Vol. 1: 47
National Education Association (NEA), Vol. 3: 49
National Firearms Act of 1934
Vol. 1: 61-62, 64, 113-114
Vol. 2: 71-72
national government, Vol. 4: 44
National Guard, Vol. 1: 46-48
National Instant Criminal Background Check System (NICS), Vol. 4: 61
National Minimum Drinking Age Act, Vol. 4: 70
National Research Council, Vol. 3: 104
National Rifle Association (NRA)
Vol. 1: 61-62, 69-71, *70*, 76, 78, 79, 94
Vol. 2: 91, 97
Vol. 3: 9, 40, 85, 86-88, *87*
Vol. 4: 15, 25, 27, 32-33, 37, *37*, *38*, 38-41
National School Safety Center, Vol. 3: 49
National Shooting Sports Foundation (NSSF)
Vol. 2: 98
Vol. 3: 31-32, 82-83
National Sportsman and Hunting and Fishing (magazine)
Vol. 2: 12-13
Vol. 4: 16
Native Americans, Vol. 1: 50, *51*
natural rights tradition, Vol. 1: 17-19, *18*
NCBH (National Coalition to Ban Handguns), Vol. 1: 78
NCVS. *See* National Crime Victimization Survey
NEA (National Education Association), Vol. 3: 49
neighbor, Vol. 3: 88-91, *90*
Nesbitt, James Dale, Vol. 3: 39, *39*
Ness, Elliot, Vol. 1: 93
New Jersey
Vol. 2: 93-94
Vol. 3: 8-9, *100*, 100
New Jersey's Fish and Game Regulations, Vol. 3: 8
New Mexico, Vol. 3: 62, 97-98
new militia movement, Vol. 1: 92-93, 95-96

New Orleans (LA), Vol. 2: 114–115
New York
Vol. 3: 99
Vol. 4: 100
New York City (NY)
Vol. 1: 97
Vol. 3: 24
New York City Police Department, Vol. 3: 82
Nichols, Terry, Vol. 1: 95–96
NICS (National Instant Criminal Background Check System), Vol. 4: 61
Nixon, Richard, Vol. 4: 21–22
Nixon, Tom, Vol. 1: 49
North Carolina, Vol. 3: 18
North Dakota, Vol. 4: 50–51
North, Simeon, Vol. 2: 19–21, *21*, 24
Novak, Jake, Vol. 3: *34*, 34
NRA. *See* National Rifle Association
NSSF. *See* National Shooting Sports Foundation
Nye Committee, Vol. 2: 72–74, *73*
Nye, Gerald, Vol. 2: 72–74, *73*

O
Oakley, Annie, Vol. 2: *11*, 11
O'Bannon, Dion, Vol. 1: 57
Ohio, Vol. 4: 57, *97*, 97, 100
Oklahoma, Vol. 3: 62
Oklahoma City bombing, Vol. 1: *95*, 95–96
Olson, Theodore, Vol. 1: 118
Olympic Games, Vol. 2: 13
Omnibus Crime Control and Law Enforcement Act of 1994, Vol. 1: 82
Omnibus Crime Control and Safe Streets Act, Vol. 1: 67
one-gun-a-month limit, Vol. 2: 90, 101–104, *103*
ordnance, Vol. 2: 125
Oregon
Vol. 3: 52
Vol. 4: 27, 56, 65
Orth, Franklin, Vol. 1: 69–70
Osburn, Carl T., Vol. 2: 13
Oswald, Lee Harvey, Vol. 1: 64–65, *65*

P
Pacino, Al, Vol. 4: 76–77
Paducah (KY), Vol. 3: 52, 114
parents, Vol. 3: 14–15, 88–91
Parents Television Council (PTC), Vol. 3: 118
Parker, Bonnie
Vol. 2: *70*
Vol. 3: 106, *106*
Parker, George (Butch Cassidy), Vol. 3: 105, *105*
Parliament, Vol. 1: 6
passenger pigeon, Vol. 1: 48
Pataki, George, Vol. 4: 32
patent arms, Vol. 2: 29–30
Patton, George, Vol. 2: 75
Pauly, Samuel, Vol. 2: 42
Payne, Doris, Vol. 4: 29, *29*
PCA (Production Code Administration)
Vol. 1: 60
Vol. 3: 107
Pearis, Mr., Vol. 1: 101
Pearl (MS), Vol. 3: 47, *47*, 52, 55–56
Pediatrics (journal), Vol. 3: 13
Pennsylvania, Vol. 3: 52, 56, 61, *61*, 62
Pennsylvania rifle, Vol. 2: 38
People v. Dukes, Vol. 3: 64–65
percussion cap, Vol. 2: 40–41
personalized guns. *See* smart guns
Pew Research Center, Vol. 4: 12
Pfeifer, Paul, Vol. 4: 100
pistol, Vol. 2: 9–10
pistols, semiautomatic, Vol. 2: 80–82, *81*, *82*
Plato, Vol. 3: 118
plinking, Vol. 2: 10
police
Vol. 1: 53–55, *54*, 66–67, 75–76
Vol. 4: 76, 77, 84
police power
Vol. 1: 105–106, 121
Vol. 3: 123
Vol. 4: 46, 124
political assassinations, Vol. 1: 64–66, *65*
political parties, Vol. 1: 72–73, *73*. *See also* Democratic Party; Republican Party
politicians, Vol. 4: 2
politics
Vol. 4:
anti-gun-control measures, 29–32, *30*
background check law, *34*, 35
Democrats/Republicans, 20–23, *21*, *22*
election of 2000, 26–27
gun control debate, 28–29, *29*
gun control, geographical element of, 32–35, *33*
gun issues move to state level, 41–42
lobbying, *37*, 37–41, *38*
party platforms of 2000, 23–26, *25*, *26*
polls *vs.* political results, 35–37
poll, Vol. 4: 2, 124
polls and guns
Vol. 4:
gender gap, *14*, 14–16
gun control measures support, *6*, 6–8
gun laws, support of, 12–13, *13*
limits of popular opinion, 16–18, *17*
problems with polls, 2–5, *3*
school shootings and, 8–11, *9*, *10*
twenty-first century, 11–12
popular culture, Vol. 1: 55–57, *56*, 59–60
Portwood, Charles, Vol. 4: 102
preemption, Vol. 4: 46–48, *47*, 124
presidential election of 2000, Vol. 4: 12, 23–27
Presser, Herman, Vol. 1: 112–113
Presser v. Illinois, Vol. 1: 112–113
Price, Carole, Vol. 2: 98–99
Printz, Jay, Vol. 1: 116
Printz v. United States, Vol. 1: 81, 116–117
prison population
Vol. 3: 24
Vol. 4: 14–15
private gun sales, Vol. 4: 51–56
Production Code Administration (PCA)
Vol. 1: 60
Vol. 3: 107
product liability. *See* manufacturer's product liability
Prohibition, Vol. 1: 57
Project ChildSafe, Vol. 3: 82
Project HomeSafe, Vol. 3: *77*, 77, *81*, 81–83
Protection of Legal Commerce in Arms Act
Vol. 2: 121–123
Vol. 4: 12, 31–32
Protestants, Vol. 1: 5–6
PTC (Parents Television Council), Vol. 3: 118
public housing, Vol. 4: 93
public opinion, Vol. 4: vii–ix, 16–18, 35–37, 97–98. *See also* polls and guns

Q
questions, poll, Vol. 4: 5
Quilici, Victor, Vol. 1: 115
Quilici v. Village of Morton Grove, Vol. 1: 115

R
race, Vol. 1: 50–52, 98
racial violence, Vol. 1: *66*, 66–67
Radical Whigs, Vol. 1: 9–10
rampage school shootings. *See* school shootings
random student gun searches, Vol. 3: 65–66
rating system, Vol. 3: 107–108, *111*, 111, *117*, 117, 118–119
Raven handgun, Vol. 3: *95*
Reagan, Ronald
Vol. 1: 73, 74
Vol. 4: 6, *21*, 23, 32
Reconstruction, Vol. 1: 52
Red Lion Area Junior High School (York, PA), Vol. 3: 61, *61*, 62
Reese, Robert, Vol. 2: 85
referendums, Vol. 4: 63–66, *65*, *66*
registration, gun
Vol. 1: 60–62, 74
Vol. 2: 71–72
Vol. 4: 13, 15, 28, 58–59
Rehnquist, William
Vol. 1: 116
Vol. 3: 58, *58*, 59
Vol. 4: 48–49
Reid, Harry, Vol. 4: 32
Remington, Vol. 2: 61, 83
Remington, Eliphalet, Vol. 2: 57
Remington Model 700, Vol. 3: 92–95, *93*
Remington, Philo, Vol. 2: 57, *61*
Remington Upland Game Hunter (video game), Vol. 3: 112
Reno, Janet, Vol. 1: 91
repeating firearms, Vol. 2: 2
repeating rifles, Vol. 2: 52–54, 57
Republican Party
Vol. 1: 72–73, 74
Vol. 4: 20–32, *21*, *22*, *25*, 33, 35, 42
The Republic (Plato), Vol. 3: 118
respondents, Vol. 4: 2, 5
revolution, right to, Vol. 1: 87–89, *89*
revolvers, Vol. 2: 9, 30–31, 44–45
Rhee, Richard, Vol. 4: 110, *110*
Richards, Ann, Vol. 4: 105
Richmond Boro Gun Club, Inc. v. City of New York, Vol. 4: 47
Ricker, Robert, Vol. 2: 112
rifle-musket, Vol. 2: 42–44, *43*, 47–50, *49*
rifles
Vol. 2:
Beecher's Bibles, 45–46
breechloaders, Vol. 2: 50–52
Browning automatic rifle, 77–78
Garand M-1 semiautomatic rifle, 74–75, *75*
history of, 36–37
"Kentucky rifle," 38
Krag-Jorgenson rifle, 62–63, *63*
M-16 rifle, 78–80, *79*
M1903 rifle, 63–64
military tactics and, 38–40, *40*
percussion cap for, 40–41
photograph of, *37*
Remington and Winchester, 57
Spencer rifle/repeating rifles, 52–54, *53*
right to bear arms. *See also* gun control legislation; Second Amendment
Vol. 1:
British Bill of Rights and, 6–8
as collective right, 84–86, *85*
before the Constitution, 2–20, *3*, *4*, *7*, *9*, *10*, *12*, *15*, *16*, *18*
riots, Vol. 1: *66*, 66–67
Robbins & Lawrence Armory, Vol. 2: 29–30
Roberti, David, Vol. 4: 67
Roberti-Roos Assault Weapons Act, Vol. 4: 67
Robinson, Tyler, Vol. 4: *115*, 115
Rodgers, Aaron, Vol. 4: 30, *30*
Romero, Gloria, Vol. 4: *68*, 68
Roosevelt, Franklin
Vol. 1: 60–61
Vol. 2: 71
Roosevelt, Theodore, Vol. 1: 47
Roos, Mike, Vol. 4: 67
Root, Elisha, Vol. 2: 32
round
Vol. 2: 125
Vol. 3: 123
Rouse, Jamie, Vol. 3: 12, *12*
Rousseau, Jean-Jacques, Vol. 1: 19
Ruby Ridge (ID), Vol. 1: 89–91, *90*
Ruger, William, Vol. 2: 85–86, *87*
Ryan, George, Vol. 3: 17, *17*

S
SAFE Colorado, Vol. 3: *41*, 41
SAFE KIDS program, Vol. 3: 81
safes, gun, Vol. 3: 76–77
safety. *See* gun safety
"sampling errors," Vol. 4: 3–4

San Diego (CA), Vol. 3: 50
Santana High School (Santee, CA), Vol. 3: 57, *57*, 62
Santee (CA), Vol. 3: 57, *57*, 62
Sarasota Herald Tribune (newspaper), Vol. 4: 52
"Saturday night specials" Vol. 2: 10, *116*, 116–117
Scalia, Antonin, Vol. 1: 116
Schnepp, Justin, Vol. 3: *51*, 51
schools
  Vol. 3:
  Columbine High School massacre, 53–55, *54*, 60–62
  Committee to Study Youth Violence, 69–70
  crimes at, 46–47
  decline of school violence, 55–56
  gangs in, 47–48, *48*
  Grunow v. Valor Corporation of Florida, 68–69, *69*
  gun-free school zones, 56–57, *57*
  guns and, 49–50
  metal detectors in, 62–65, *63*, *64*
  rampage school shootings, *47*, 50–53, *51*
  random student gun searches, 65–66
  safe gun storage at home, 66–68, *67*
  teenagers carrying guns in, 28
  United States v. Lopez, 48–49, *58*, 58–60, *61*
school shootings
  Vol. 1: 101–102
  Vol. 3:
  access to guns and, 11
  at Fair Park High School, *vii*, vii
  by Jamie Rouse, Stephen Abbott, *12*, 12
  Columbine High School massacre, 53–55, *54*, 60–62
  in Red Lion (PA), *61*, 61
  in West Paducah (KY), 114
  rampage school shootings, 46–47, *47*, 50–53, *51*
  safe firearms storage and, 66–68, *67*
  shock from, ix
  statistics/incidents, 49–50
  violence in media and, 121–122
  violence in video games and, 112–113
  Vol. 4: 8–11, *9*, *10*, 28–29, 67
school zone
  Vol. 3: 124
  Vol. 4: 124
Schroeder, Pat, Vol. 3: 96, *96*
Schumer, Charles, Vol. 4: *17*, 17, 35, 70
Scotland, Vol. 3: 56
Scott, Winfield, Vol. 1: 44
Second Amendment
  Vol. 1:
  adaptability of, 38
  alternative wording of, 34–35
  Congressional debates over, 36
  debate over, vii–viii, xii–xiii
  gun control and, 82
  historical conditions that led to, 2–20, *3*, *7*, *9*, *10*, *12*, *15*, *16*, *18*
  historical question about, x
  judicial view of 104–119, *105*, *109*, *111*
  limited impact of, 37
  militia and, 43
  modern debate over 84–102, *85*, *89*, *90*, *92*, *95*, *100*
  NRA and, 71
  racial question about, 50–52
  "to keep and bear arms," 36–37
  U.S. Supreme Court and, *xiii–xiv*
  Vol. 4: vii–viii, 30–31, 45–46, 118–119
Second Amendment Sisters, Inc., Vol. 4: *44*, 44, 89, *89*, *90*, 90, 108, *108*, 119, *119*, *120*, 120
Seegars v. Ashcroft, Vol. 4: 31
Segro, Eugene, Vol. 3: 61
select militia, Vol. 1: 121
self-defense
  Vol. 1: 2, 86–87, 121
  Vol. 2: 10, 125
  Vol. 3: 31–32, 79–80, 124
  Vol. 4:
  Bernhard Goetz, 77–79, *78*
  carrying weapons and, *86*
  concealed weapons and, 106–109, *107*, *108*
  defined, 124
  guns and, 81–83, *82*
  in twenty-first century, 94
  justifiable homicide, 79–81
  NCVS figures and, 86–87
  weapon use and violent crime, 88–90
  women/justifiable homicide, *90*, 90–92
semiautomatic guns, Vol. 2: *2*, 3
semiautomatic pistols, Vol. 2: 80–82, *81*, *82*
semiautomatic weapon
  Vol. 2: 125
  Vol. 3: 124
  Vol. 4: 124
Senate Governmental Affairs Committee, Vol. 3: *111*, 111
September 11, 2001, terrorist attacks
  Vol. 1: 99–101
  Vol. 4: 118
Serpico (film), Vol. 4: 76–77
Serpico, Frank, Vol. 4: *76*, 76–77
7th Annual Gun Turn In, Vol. 4: 33
sexual violence, Vol. 3: 115
shall-issue states, Vol. 4: 99–100, 106
Shan, Zhang, Vol. 4: 16
Sharps, Christian, Vol. 2: 45
Sharpton, Al, Vol. 3: *2*, 2
Shaw, Lemuel, Vol. 1: 106
Shaw, Thomas, Vol. 2: 40–41
Shays's Rebellion
  Vol. 1: 22–23, *23*, 41–42
  Vol. 2: 18
Sheets, James, Vol. 3: *61*, 61
Shoemake, Larry, Vol. 3: *93*, 93
shooting, Vol. 2: 10–12, *11*
Shooting Industry (gun industry publication), Vol. 2: 88
single-shot guns, Vol. 2: 2
Sitz, Michigan Department of State Police v., Vol. 3: 65
skeet, Vol. 2: 12–13
slavery, Vol. 1: 30, 32, 50–52
Sliwa, Stephen, Vol. 3: 89, *89*
small arms, Vol. 2: 2
smart guns
  Vol. 2: *91*, 91–94
  Vol. 3: *89*, 89, 96, *96*, 98–102, *99*, 124
Smith & Wesson
  Vol. 2: 55–56, 61, 83–84, 87, 92, 117–120, *118*
  Vol. 3: 101, 102
Smith, Franklin, Vol. 1: 15–16
Smith, Kevin, Vol. 4: 25, *25*
Smith, Laura, Vol. 3: *111*, 111
Smith, Sean, Vol. 3: 97–98
Smith v. Bryco Arms, Vol. 3: 97–98
Spencer, Brenda, Vol. 3: *29*, 29
Spencer, Christopher, Vol. 2: 52–53
sport hunting, Vol. 3: 4–8, *5*, *6*
Springfield Armory, Vol. 2: 7, 17–18, 24–26, *25*, 28–29, 41, 54–55, 63, 85
Springfield Model 1855 rifle-musket, Vol. 2: 43–44
Springfield (OR), Vol. 3: 52, 53
standing army, Vol. 1: 9–10, 16–17, 24, 121
Staples v. United States, Vol. 1: 118–119
state Bills of Rights
  Vol. 1: 32–34
  Vol. 4: *49*, 49–51, *50*
state courts, Vol. 1: 107–108
state governments
  Vol. 1: 105–106
  Vol. 4:
  California's gun regulations, 66–69, *68*, *71*
  CCW laws of, 96–100, 111–112
  "gun show loophole" and, 55–56
  gun shows on publicly owned property, 56–58, *57*
  laboratory of the states, 69–72
  powers of, 44–46
  preemption, 46–48, *47*
  referendums, 63–66, *65*, *66*
  registration of guns, 58–59
  waiting periods, 60–63, *62*
states, Vol. 1: 28–30, 108–110
Stearns, Cliff, Vol. 4: 98
Steinhauser, Robert, Vol. 3: 56
Stevens, John Paul
  Vol. 1: 116
  Vol. 3: 121
Stockton (CA), Vol. 3: 51
Stoner, Eugene, Vol. 2: 78
Stop Handgun Violence group, Vol. 3: 30, *30*
storage of firearms
  Vol. 3:
  child access prevention laws, 16–19
  children and, ix
  firearms education, 85–86
  gun locks, *73*, *77*, 77–80, *78*
  gun safes, 76–77
  Project HomeSafe, *81*, 81–83
  school shootings and, 66–68, *67*
  suicide and, 40–42, *41*
  unsafe storage, *73*, 73–76, *74*
Straff, Ron, Vol. 4: *49*, 49
Stubblefield, James, Vol. 2: 23
student searches, Vol. 3: 62–66, *63*
Students Working Against Depression (SWAD), Vol. 3: 34
Sturm, Alexander, Vol. 2: 85
Sturm, Ruger & Company
  Vol. 2: 85–86, *86*, 87, 93
  Vol. 3: 97, 101
Sturm, Ruger's Old Model Single Action Revolver, Vol. 3: 91–92
submachine gun, Vol. 2: 68–70, *69*, 71
"subway vigilante," Vol. 4: 77–79, *78*
suicide
  Vol. 2: 93
  Vol. 3: viii–ix, 16, 22, 32–42, *34*, *37*, *39*, 49, 53, 55, 72, 124
  Vol. 4: 89, 90, 124
Sullivan Law
  Vol. 1: 57
  Vol. 2: 69
supremacy clause, Vol. 4: 44
Supreme Court. *See* U.S. Supreme Court
SWAD (Students Working Against Depression), Vol. 3: 34

T

Taber, Alberta (Canada), Vol. 3: 56
Talcott, George, Vol. 2: 24–25
Taney, Roger, Vol. 1: 50–51
Taurus International
  Vol. 2: 92
  Vol. 3: 98
teachers, Vol. 3: 60
teenagers. *See* schools; youth violence
Telecommunications Act of 1996, Vol. 3: *119*
television
  Vol. 1: 64
  Vol. 3: 104–106, 108–110, *112*, 113–121, *119*
Tennessee
  Vol. 3: 52
  Vol. 4: 100
Tennessee state court, Vol. 1: 107–108
Texas, Vol. 4: 96–97, 105
Thomas, Clarence, Vol. 1: 116
Thompson, John, Vol. 2: 68–70, *69*
Thompson submachine gun (tommy gun), Vol. 2: 68–70, *69*, 71
Thoreau, Henry David, Vol. 4: 121
Tiananmen Square (China), Vol. 1: *89*, 89
Time magazine, Vol. 4: 7–8
Tinker v. Des Moines, Vol. 3: 63
T.L.O. case, Vol. 3: 63–64
Tomkins, Vol. 2: 119–120
Tone Loc, Vol. 3: *25*
Torrio, Johnny, Vol. 1: 57
Townshend Acts of 1767, Vol. 1: 13
trapshooting, Vol. 2: 12
Trenchard, John, Vol. 1: 10
trigger locks
  Vol. 2: 98–101, *99*, *100*
  Vol. 3: *18*, *77*, 77–83, *78*, *81*, 124
  Vol. 4: 13, 15, 28, 124
Twain, Mark, Vol. 2: 31–32

U
Understanding and Preventing Violence (National Research Council), Vol. 3: 104
Uniform Crime Reporting (UCR) program, Vol. 4: 83–84
Uniform Militia Act of 1792, Vol. 1: 40–41
United Nations (UN) Convention on the Rights of the Child, Vol. 3: 3
United States, Vol. 2: 5–6
United States Revolver Association, Vol. 1: 58
United States v. Cruikshank, Vol. 1: 110–112, *111*
United States v. Emerson
Vol. 1: xiv, 117–118
Vol. 4: 31
United States v. Lopez
Vol. 3: *58*, 58–60
Vol. 4: 48–49
United States v. Miller, Vol. 1: xiv, 62, 109, 113–115
University of California, Santa Barbara, Vol. 3: 108
unlicensed sellers, Vol. 4: 53–55
unsafe guns, Vol. 3: 91–98, *93*, *95*
U.S. Army
Vol. 1: 45, 50
Vol. 2: 62–67, 78–80, *79*
U.S. Army Ordnance Department, Vol. 2: 26–27
U.S. Congress
Vol. 1: 24–25, 36, 52
Vol. 3: 56–57, 59
Vol. 4: 11, 12, 27, 29–32
U.S. Constitution
Vol. 1: xiii–xiv, 22–30, *26*, *28*, 38, 104
Vol. 3: 2
Vol. 4: 44–46, 117
U.S. Department of Justice. *See also* National Crime Victimization Survey
Vol. 3: 82
Vol. 4: vii, 83–84
U.S. Fish and Wildlife Service, Vol. 3: 6–7, 8
U.S. government, Vol. 2: 17
U.S. House of Representatives, Vol. 4: 29, 31
U.S. military, Vol. 2: 76–77
U.S. Secret Service, Vol. 3: 11
U.S. Supreme Court
Vol. 1: 50–51, 104, 107, 109–119, *114*
Vol. 3: *58*, 58–60, 63–64, 121
Vol. 4: 45–46, 48–49
U.S. Surgeon General, Vol. 3: 113

V
Valor Corporation, Vol. 3: 68–69
V-chip, Vol. 3: 118, 121
video games, Vol. 3: 110–113, *111*
Vielle, Paul, Vol. 2: 57
vigilante, Vol. 4: 77
violence. *See also* youth violence
Vol. 3:
guns in movies/television, 108–110, *109*
in mass media, 104–108, *105*, *112*
in mass media, solutions, 116–119
in video games, 110–113, *111*
Telecommunications Act of 1996, *119*, 120–121
violent media, effects of, 113–116
Violence Policy Center (VPC), Vol. 3: 87–88
violent crime
Vol. 3: 23
Vol. 4: 74, *85*, 88–90, 94
Virginia
Vol. 1: 30–31
Vol. 2: 102
Vol. 3: 18
Virginians Against Handgun Violence, Vol. 3: 83, *83*
Volkmer, Harold, Vol. 1: 75
VPC (Violence Policy Center), Vol. 3: 87–88

W
Waco (TX), Vol. 1: 91, *92*
Wadsworth, Decius, Vol. 2: 26
Waite, Morrison, Vol. 1: 110
waiting periods
Vol. 1: 78–79
Vol. 4: *60*, 60–63, *62*, 124
Walden (Thoreau), Vol. 4: 121
Waldorf, James, Vol. 2: 117
Wall Street Journal, Vol. 3: 56
Wal-Mart, Vol. 4: *62*, 62–63
War of 1812
Vol. 1: 42–45, *44*
Vol. 2: 39
Washington
Vol. 3: 52, 111
Vol. 4: 64
Washington, D.C., Vol. 1: *44*, 44–45
Washington, George
Vol. 1: *10*, 17, 20, *28*, 42
Vol. 2: 17, 19
Waters, Asa, Vol. 2: 20–21
Watts riot, Vol. 1: 67
weapons charges, Vol. 3: 28
weapon use, Vol. 4: 88–90
Weaver, Randy, Vol. 1: 89–91, 95
Webb, Allyson, Vol. 4: *29*, 29
Webster, Daniel, Vol. 4: 106–107
Weiss, Douglas, Vol. 3: *99*, 99
Weiss, Hymie, Vol. 1: 57–58
West Paducah (KY), Vol. 3: 52
Westside Middle School, Vol. 3: 52
West, The, Vol. 1: 49–50, 55–56
Whiskey Rebellion, Vol. 1: 42, *43*, 93
Whitehill, Robert, Vol. 1: 32
White League, Vol. 1: 110–112
Whitney, Eli, Vol. 2: 17, 21–23, *22*
Williams, Eli, Vol. 3: 43
Wilson, Eddie, Vol. 3: 93, *93*
Winchester, Vol. 2: 84
Winchester, Oliver, Vol. 2: 57
Winchester Repeating Arms Company, Vol. 2: 57
Winthrop, John, Vol. 1: 10–11
Wisconsin, Vol. 4: 50, 64
Wolbrink, Mike, Vol. 4: *103*, 103
Wolcott, Oliver, Vol. 2: 21, 22
women, Vol. 4: 9, 14–16, *90*, 90–92, *93*, 93
Women Against Gun Control, Vol. 4: 16
Woodham, Luke, Vol. 3: 52
Woods, William B., Vol. 1: 112–113
World War II, Vol. 2: 76
World War I, Vol. 2: 67–68
Wyoming, Vol. 4: 100

Y
Young v. Bryco, Vol. 2: 112–113
Youth Handgun Safety Act, Vol. 3: 85
youth violence
Vol. 3:
accidental shootings involving children, 42–43
children as killers, *30*, 30
comparison with other countries, 32–33, *33*
decrease in 1990s, *23*, 23–24
gangs and guns, 24–26, *25*
handguns and, *26*, 26–27
rates of, 22
safe storage of firearms, 40–42, *41*, *42*
self-defense by children, 31–32
statistics, 43–44
suicide, *34*, 34–40, *37*, *39*
teenagers carrying guns, 27–29, *29*
young people as victims, 31

Z
Zangara, Giuseppe
Vol. 1: 61
Vol. 2: 71
Zien, David, Vol. 4: *98*, 98
Zinzo, Jedaiah D., Vol. 3: *51*, 51